THREE LEWY BODIES
PORTRAYING DEMENTIA

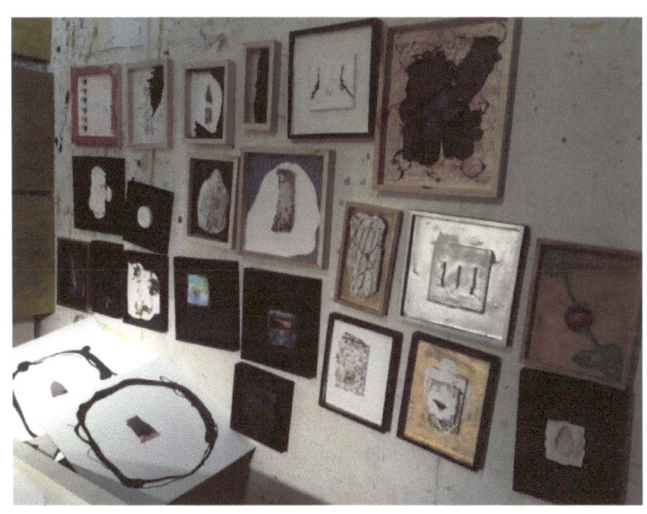

Gary Walters

ISBN 978-1505860467

Vector Print and Publishing

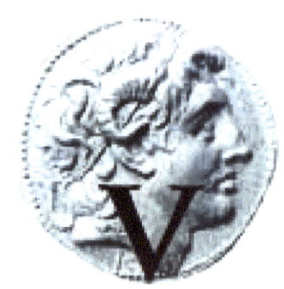

There can be few experiences more

daunting then the experience of

dementia. In those who have dementia, the slow loss of cognition and memory is an agony and anticipation until memory and body gradually lose their function. In those

who must watch and care for the afflicted, it is a slow loss of connection with those closest to us which we are

powerless to prevent or alter.

The approaches of dementia are insidious. Alzheimer's is a word that can strike a fear in us even more

devastating than cancer. Less well know and less frequently diagnosed is Lewy Body Disease. Early on it is difficult often impossible to diagnose a dementia and the denial of a diagnosis is often, as in my case, fierce. There is currently no cure and really nothing that affects the progress of the disease.

Thus we explain away the little losses of memory, the disorientation, the decline of interest in things, the attempts to hide or disguise confusion, until it can't any longer be ignored. And then there are the medical consultations. And then there is the dawning realization that dementia is happening and all that can be done is almost nothing.

In my case, the denial lasted three years and then a fall suddenly caused in some way a collapse in Peter's fairly steady condition which in Lewy Body Disease includes Parkinsonian symptoms as well as cognitive decline. It attacks the brain not through the accumulation of plaque but rather through the over production of protein in the cells of the brain, eventually killing them. It proceeds on a different pathway, often attacking motor neurons before the seats of memory, language and reason. But it does attack these as well and, as in Alzheimer's, this is a non curable and fatal disease.

The works in this installation were made during the summer and early fall of 2014. The impulse to make them coincided with first the hospitalization of Peter and then his move to long term care.

My responses to these events and the preceding months of travel and Peter's catastrophic fall during that travel have been published in a collection of writing and illustrations titled *The Shock of Parting* to which this installation is a companion volume.

Both the writing and the pieces in this installation reflect my shock, grief, and dismay at the upheaval in our lives and the appallingly rapid changes in Peter's condition. I only realized in retrospect my refusal to accept the changes caused by the advance of a dementia and the ensuing frantic search for some way to alleviate this condition. And so the full impact of a fateful change was all the more severe

The art work in this group of pieces was not a catharsis, for grief has a weight and an ungraspable, labyrinthine life of its own. But it was a way to let my emotions find some sort of correlative, some sort of expression. Like all such powerful and irremediable changes in our lives, we want somehow to counter the attack and to make something of suffering that is positive and relates us to others.

In making these pieces, I grabbed onto whatever came to hand or to mind in the studio. I became somewhat demented myself. I wanted to participate with and mirror what I imagined Peter was experiencing. I had the strangest sense that he was entering another state of existence, one with merit and value in the whole range of our human place in the world. He has been I can only say at peace with the changes he undergoes, accepting with grace and often his old familiar wit and humor his life in care. This is a blessing for me amidst all the rest.

I felt there was a shamanistic identification with the illness and indeed art making has much in common with shamanistic rite. But the wild ride over, I would fall back to earth, grief still largely present, and no magical cure discovered.

I used every sort of material about me in the studio and poured out, squeezed out the paint. There was no patience – a kind of rage of making- pausing for memories shaken out and the tears bidden and unbidden. Texts, maps, photos, and other indicators or time and place and realization underlie the surfaces of these pieces which I for the most part needed to cover up, to bury, to forget, to come to terms with, to nullify, for memory lost to my companion was painful for me. Or I was portraying the slow and deadly eradication of memory in Peter's brain. I was trying to portray the paths of nerves, the shooting of these faster than light impulses, and the blockages being encountered. I made little arrangements of wires, little power stations. I used sea shells as signs of encrustation and plastic material calcified. I conjoined what could never otherwise be joined and tore apart all maps all poems all drawings all texts.

The parts very deliberately do not form any expected whole and what the condition of dementia is remains a mystery exacting close attention, the very best of our compassion, and courage before the slow but certain death of a loved one with whom we cannot communicate.

To those of you who look at these pieces, I hope for connection with your own sense of how dementia might feel, or what it has been like for you, and, more broadly, how it might be a reflection of this very present on planet Earth.

The works are presented more or less in the order they were made understanding that there was much backing and forthing and toing and froing but very little hemming and hawing. Also the titles have been added just now as I write this introduction. It feels, as always with titles for works of visual art, like something at once artificial and yet helpful for language really does come from a different part of the brain and in this case a later moment. They are a gloss on the pieces and they suggest a coherence where the real subject is the breakdown of that fragile ephemeral thing we call consciousness.

Hastings, Ontario

December 31, 2014

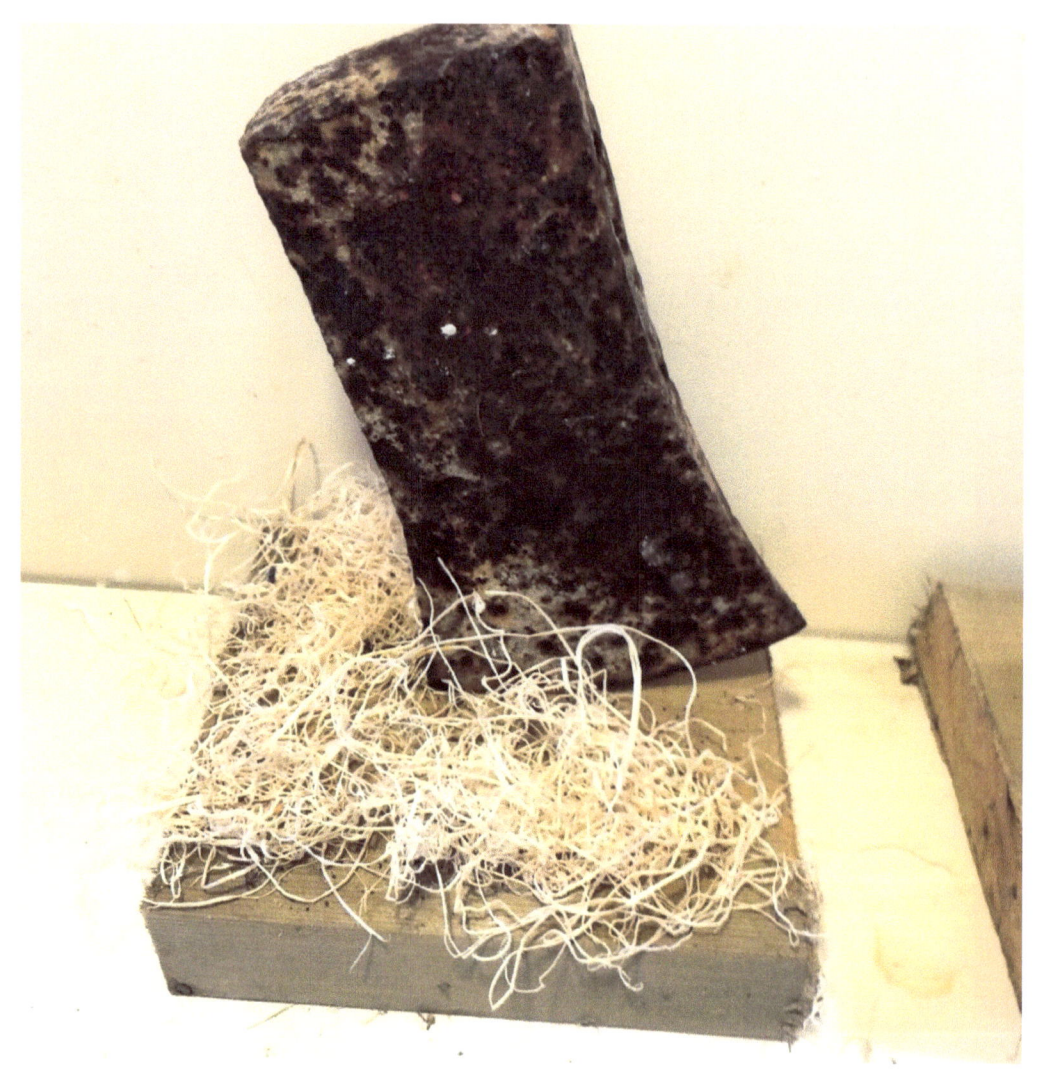

strike

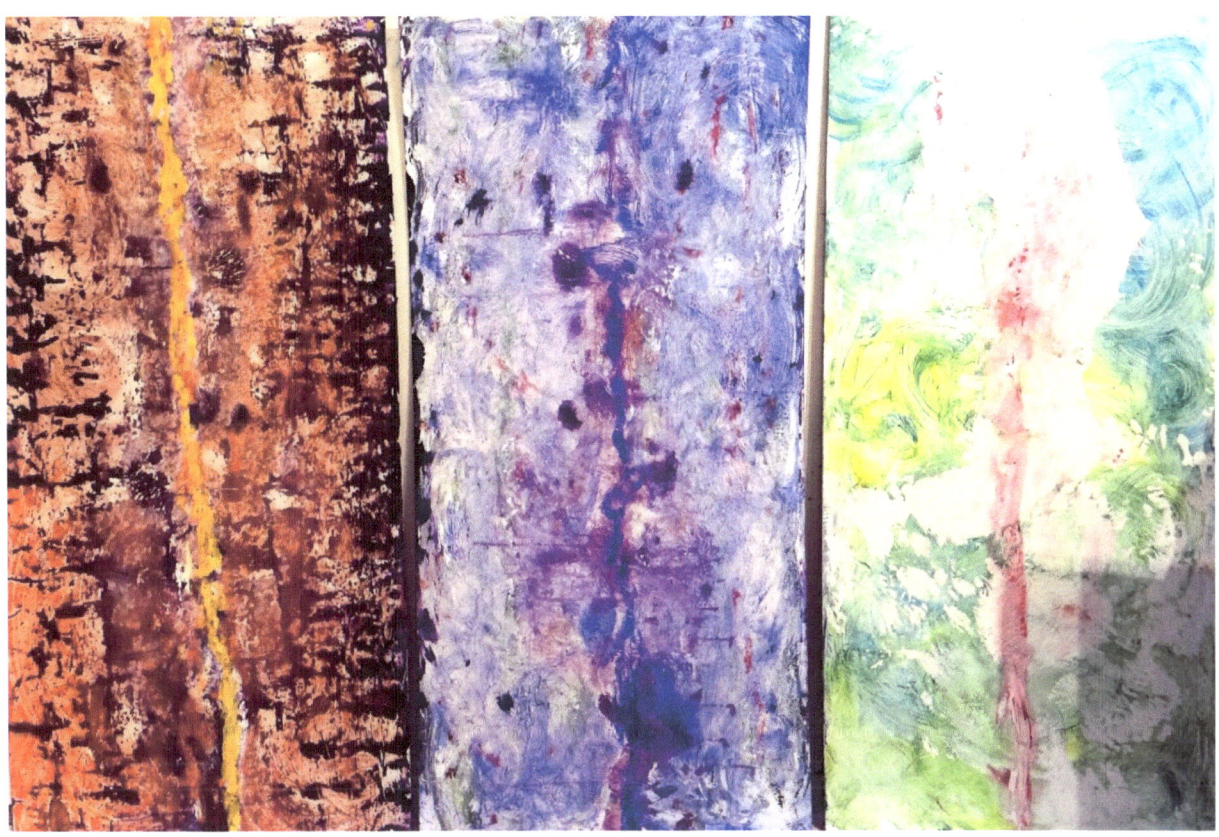

triptych showing three different emotional states of the brain

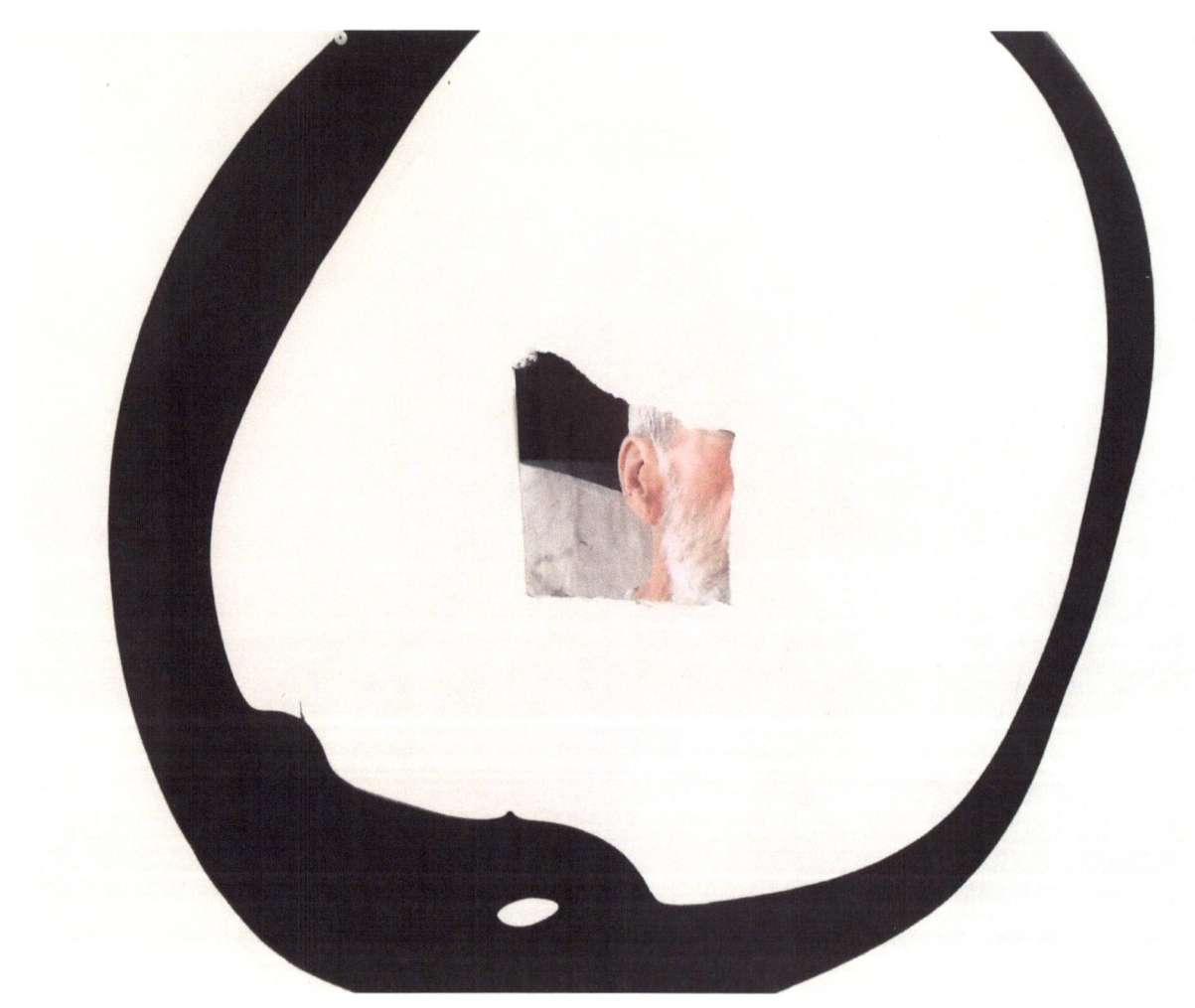

peter hearing

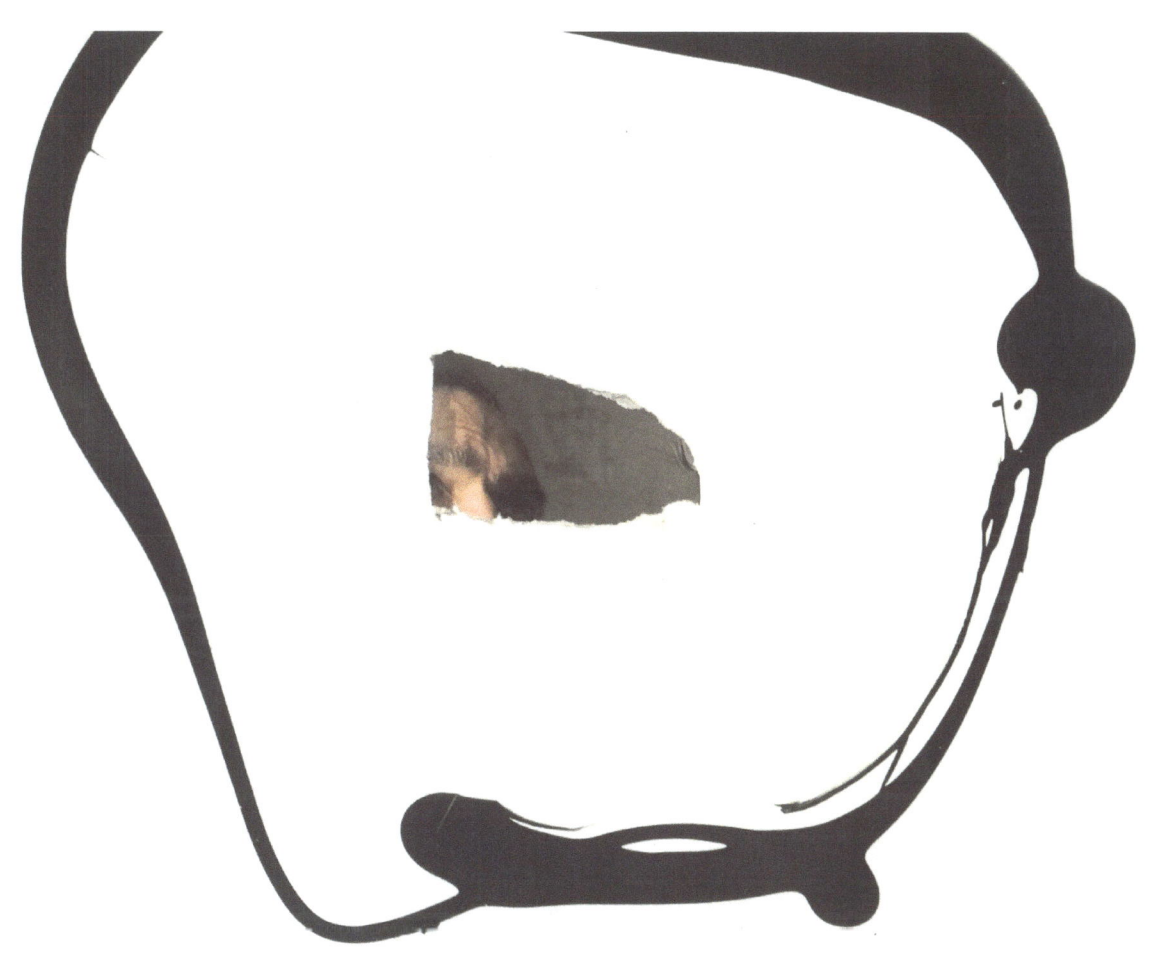

peter thinking

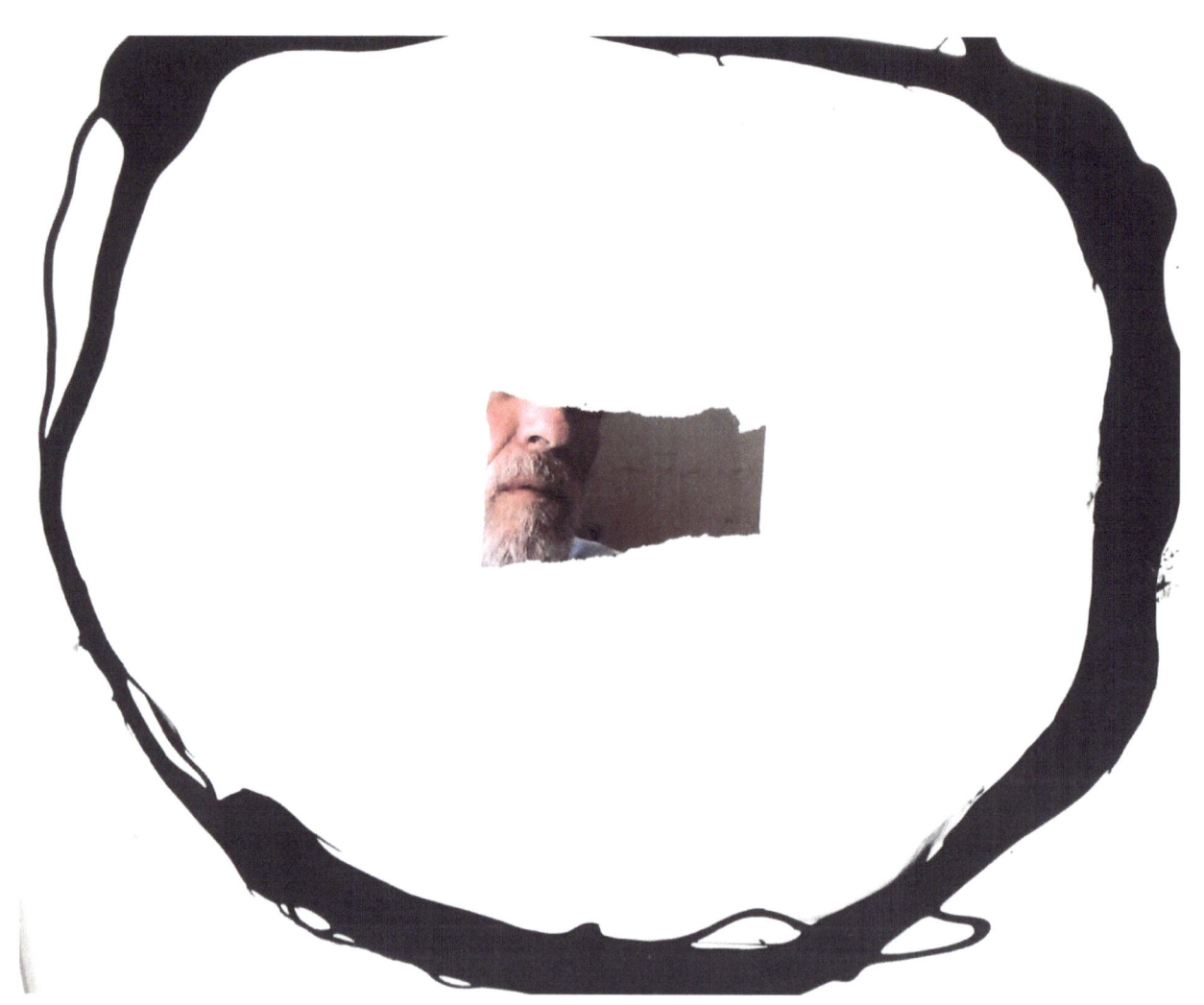

peter has no sense of smell

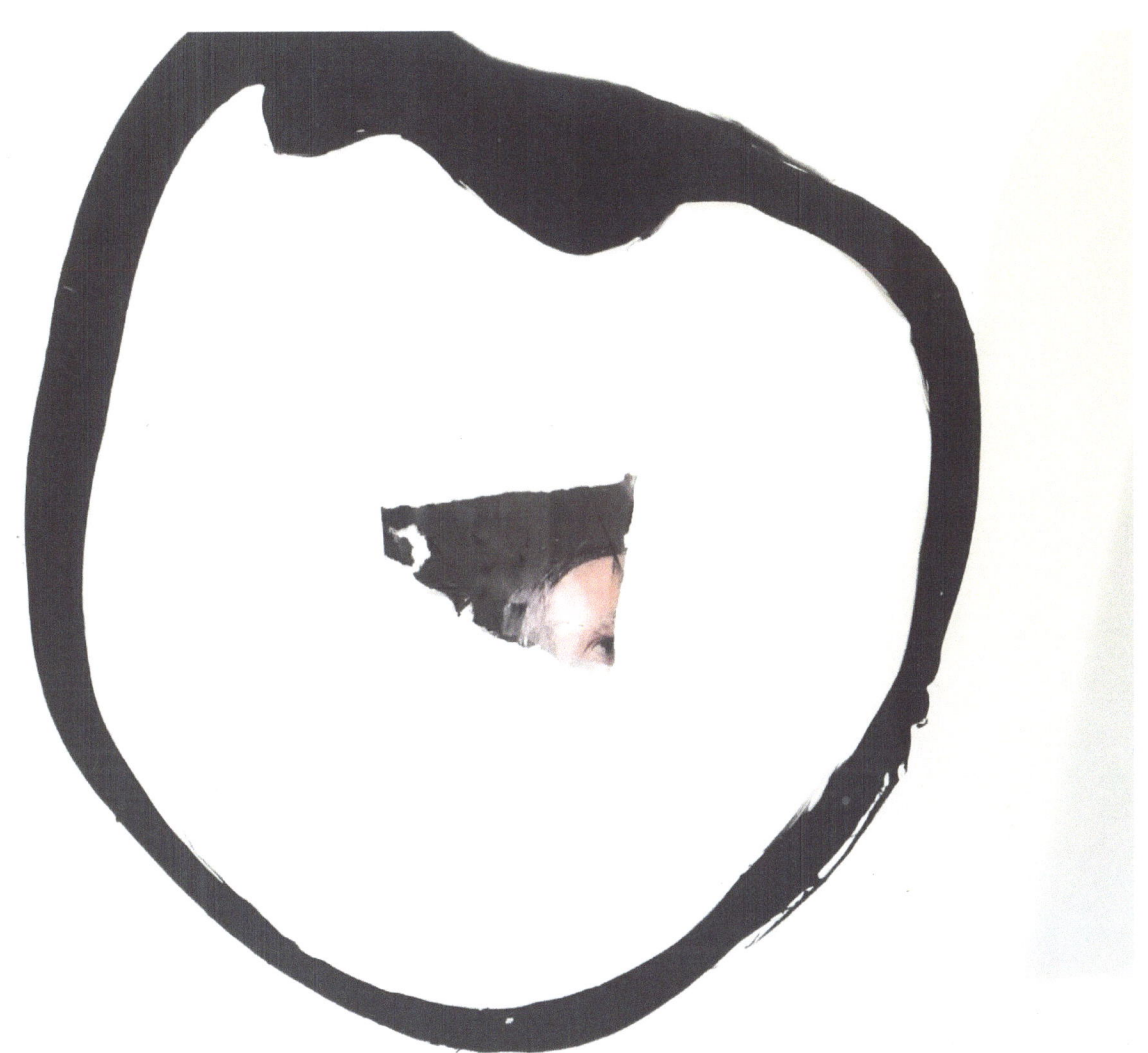

peter seeing

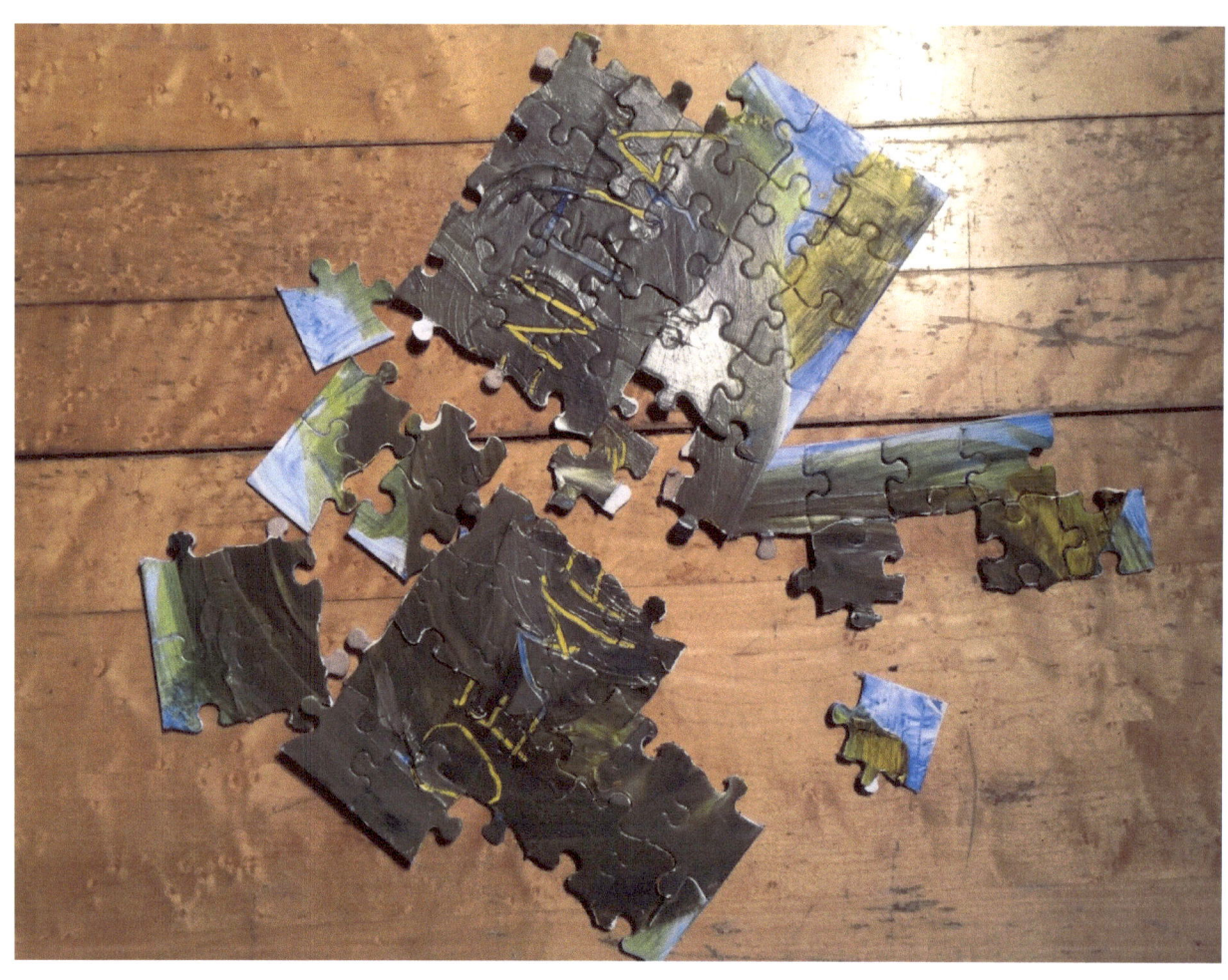

dementia puzzle itself undone

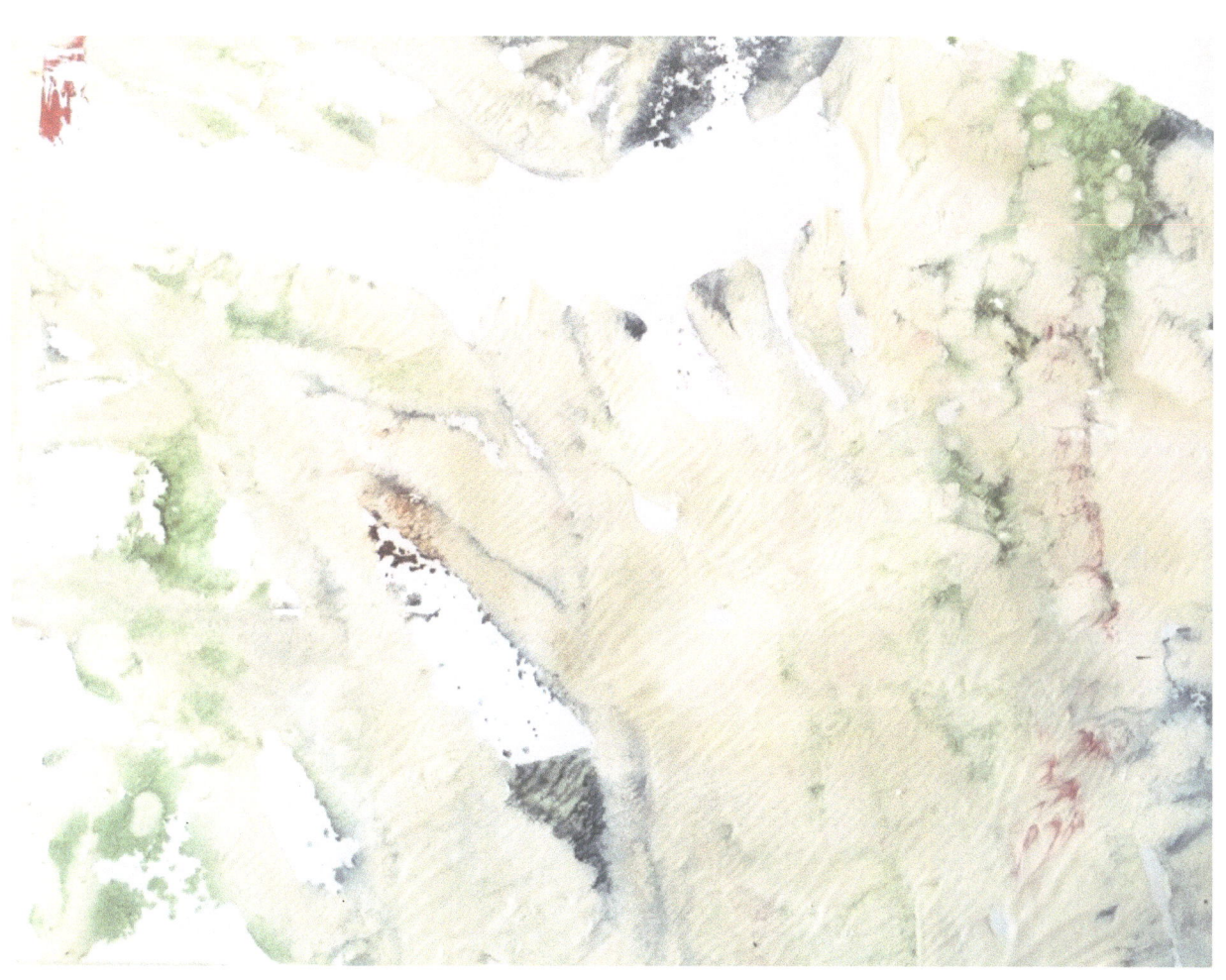

i try to feel you

this is where I was born

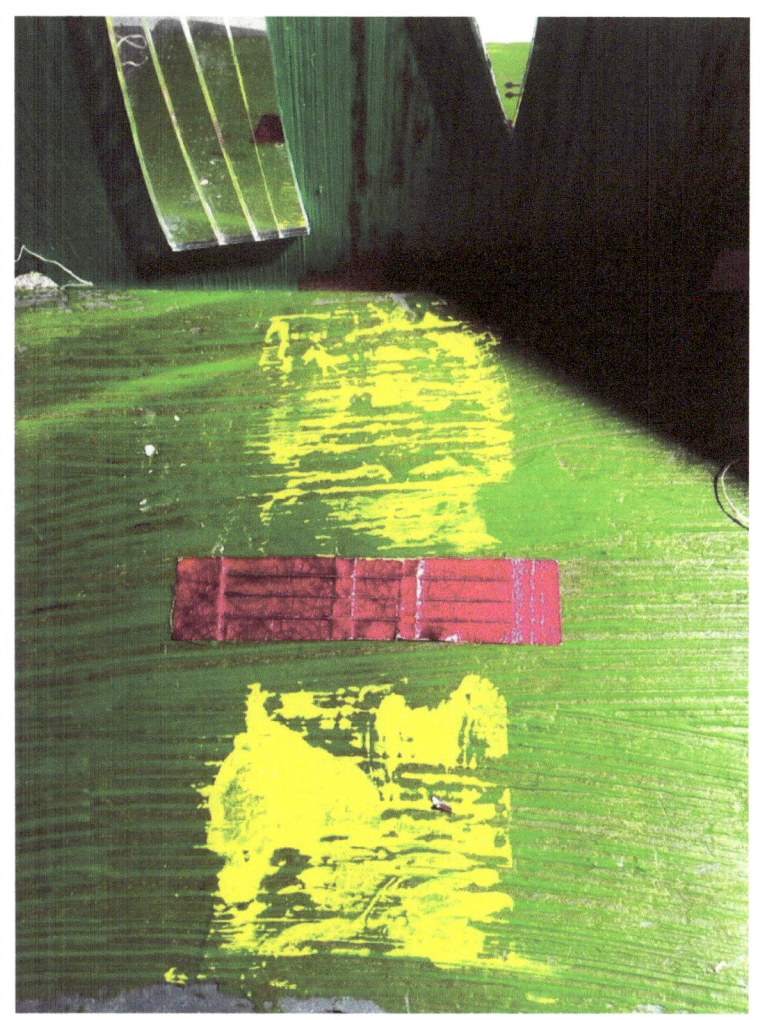

landscape with pink pins

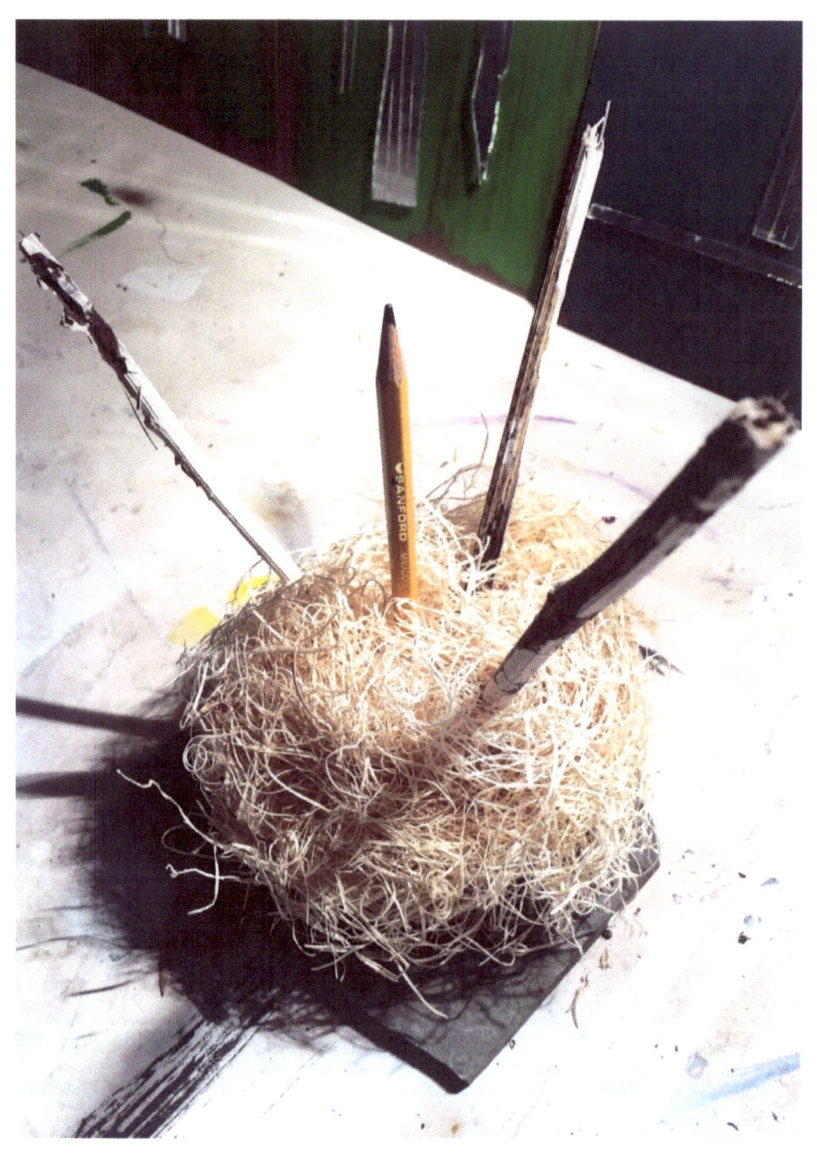

the brain is pierced to no avail

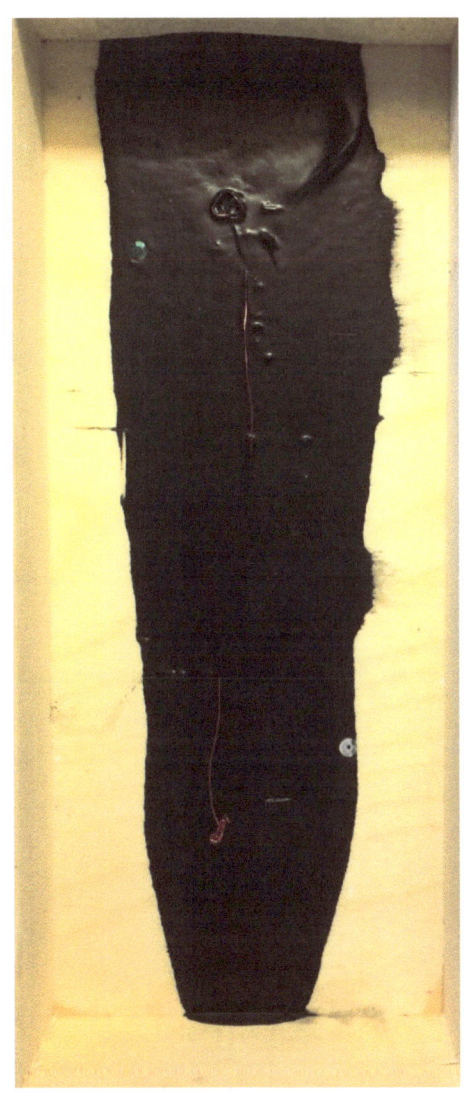

i am drowning

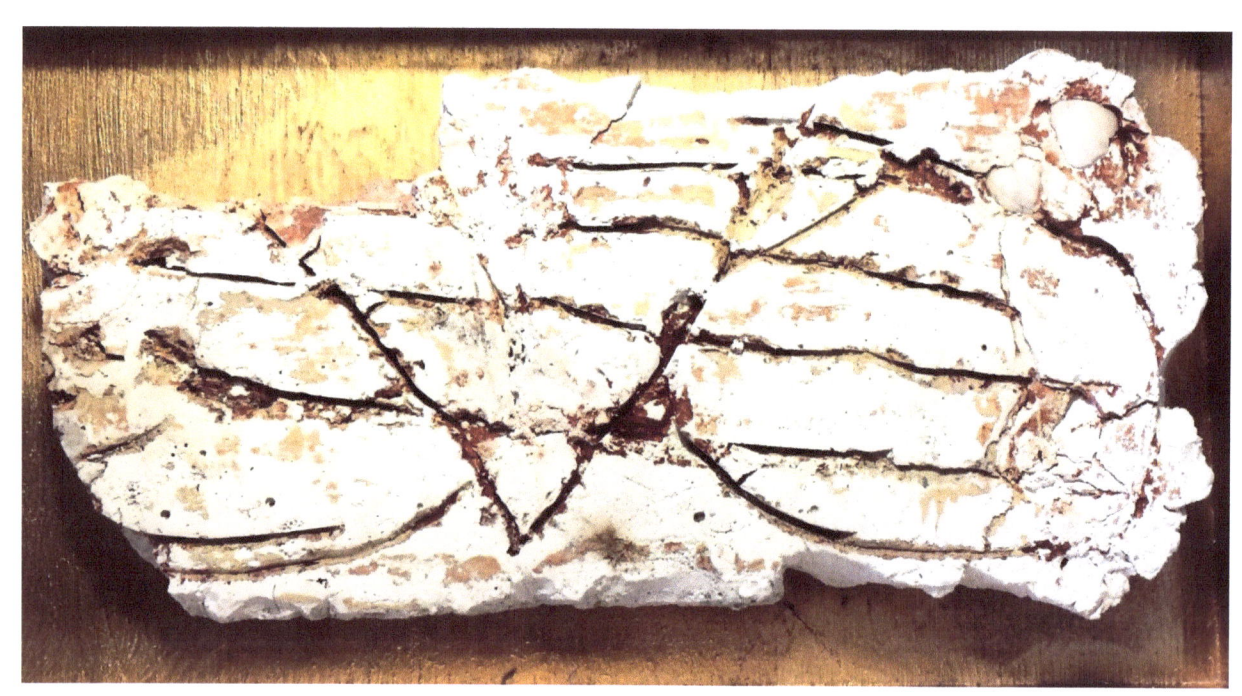

which way do we go

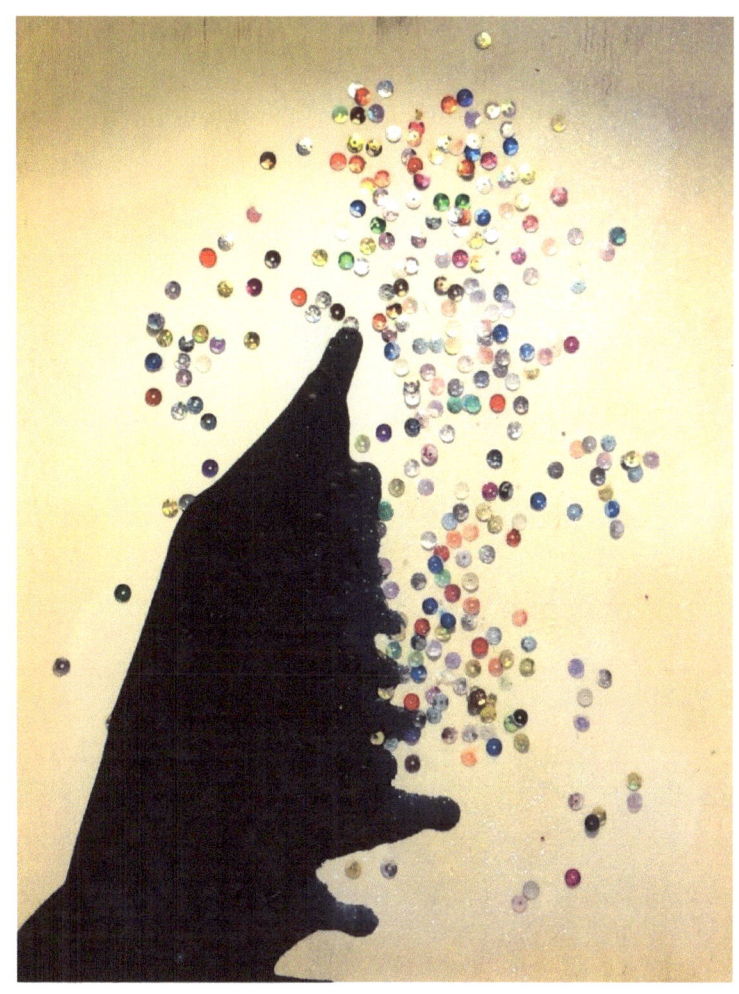

scattering brightness

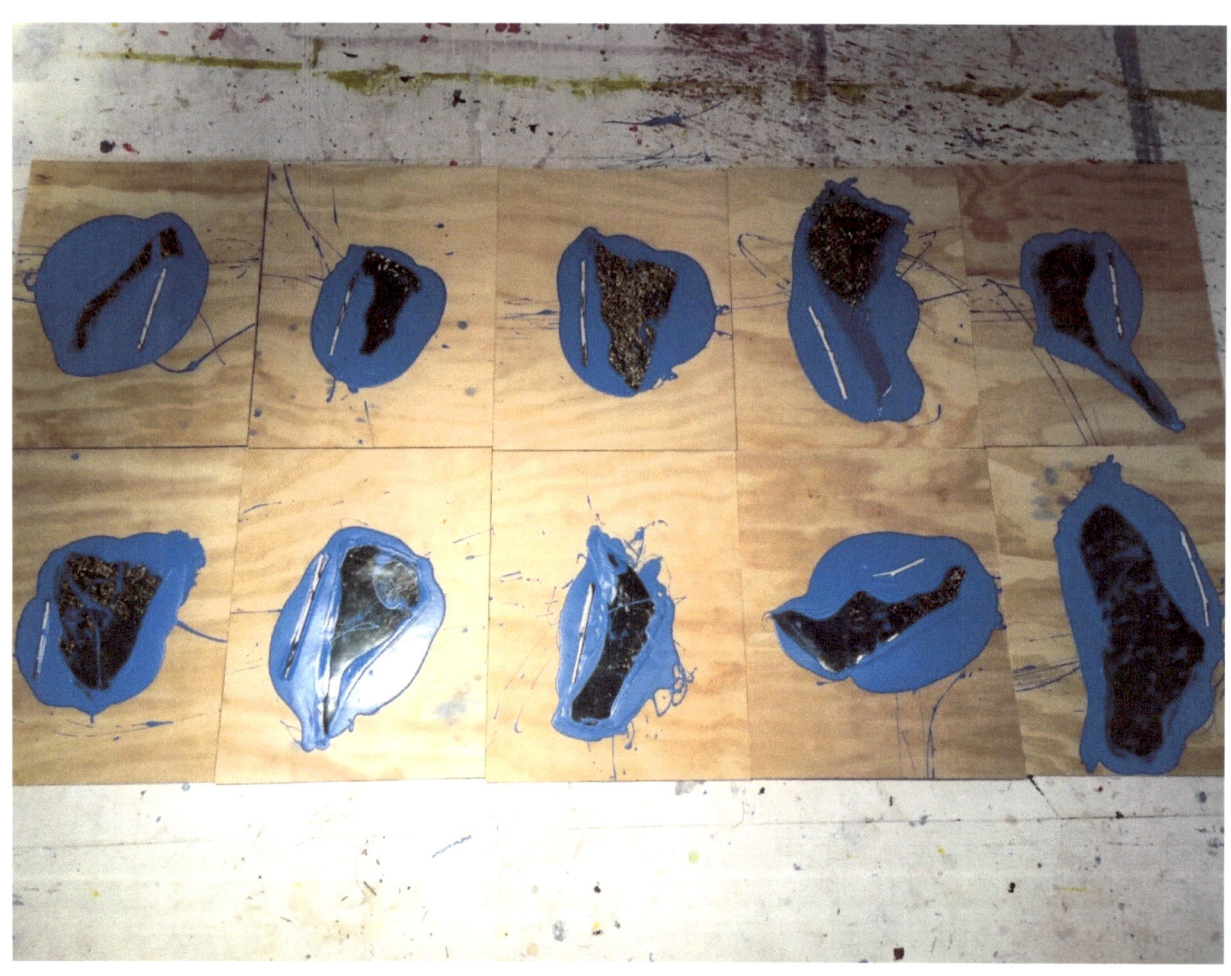

on the lake beside the river before my house

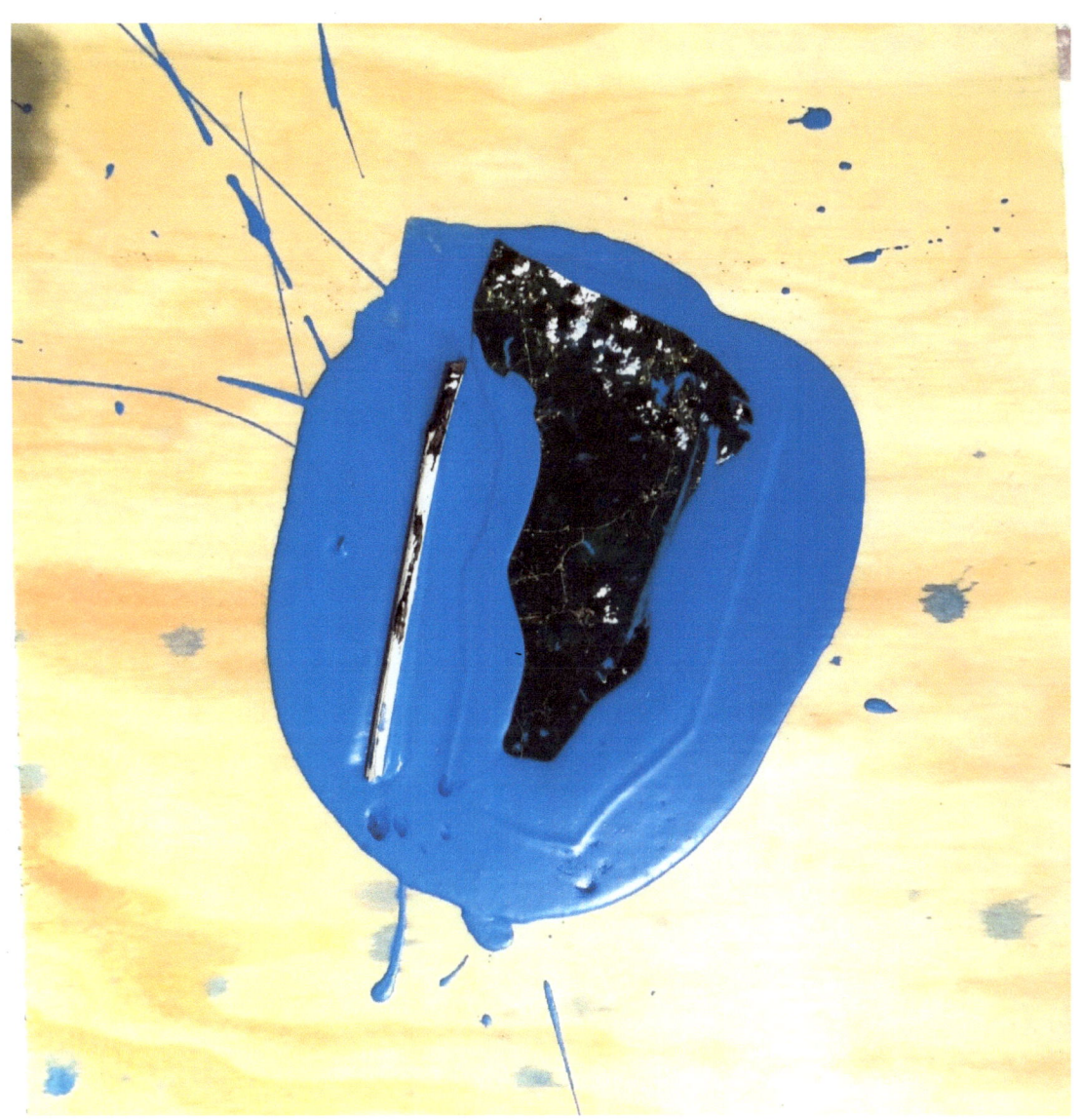

i float with you

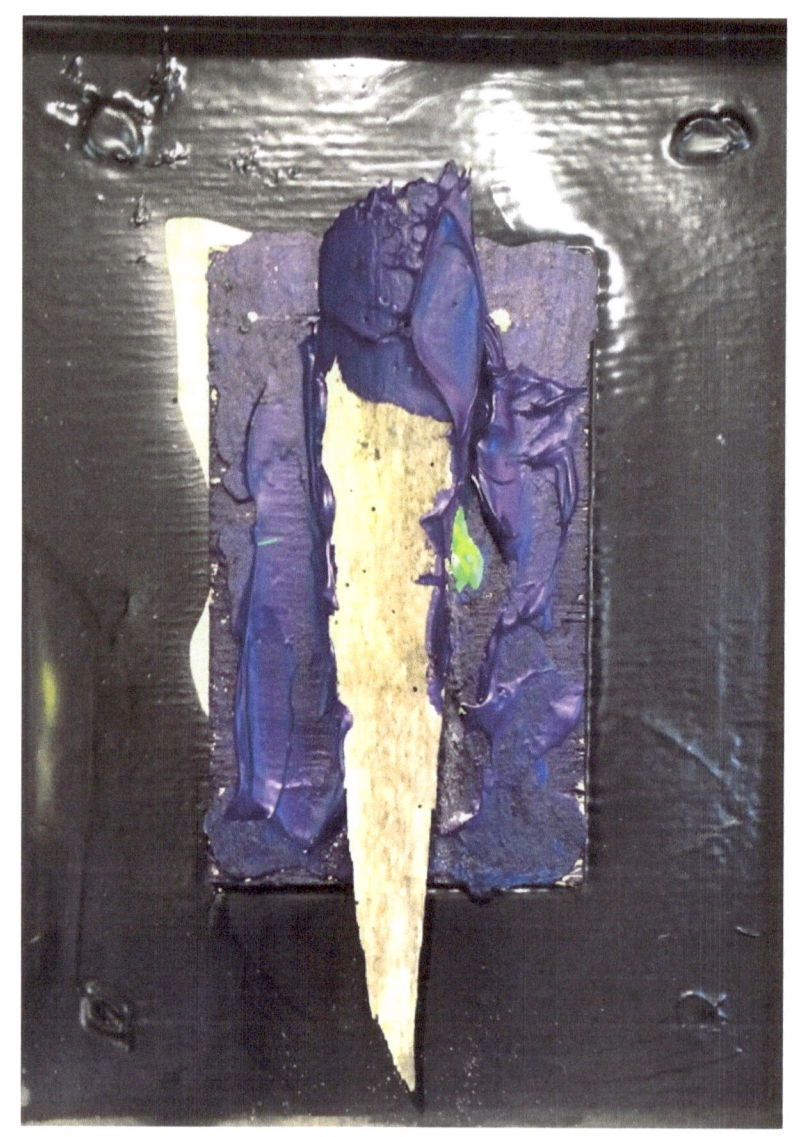

the deeper reaches of grief

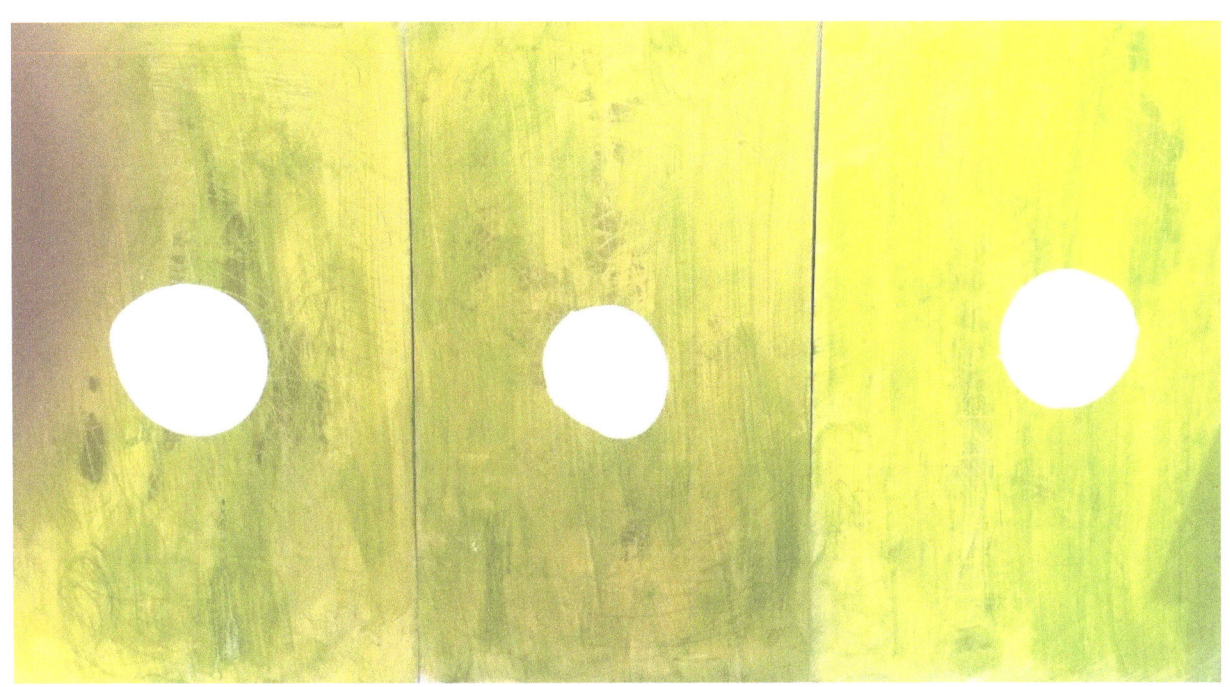

three Lewy Bodies like holes

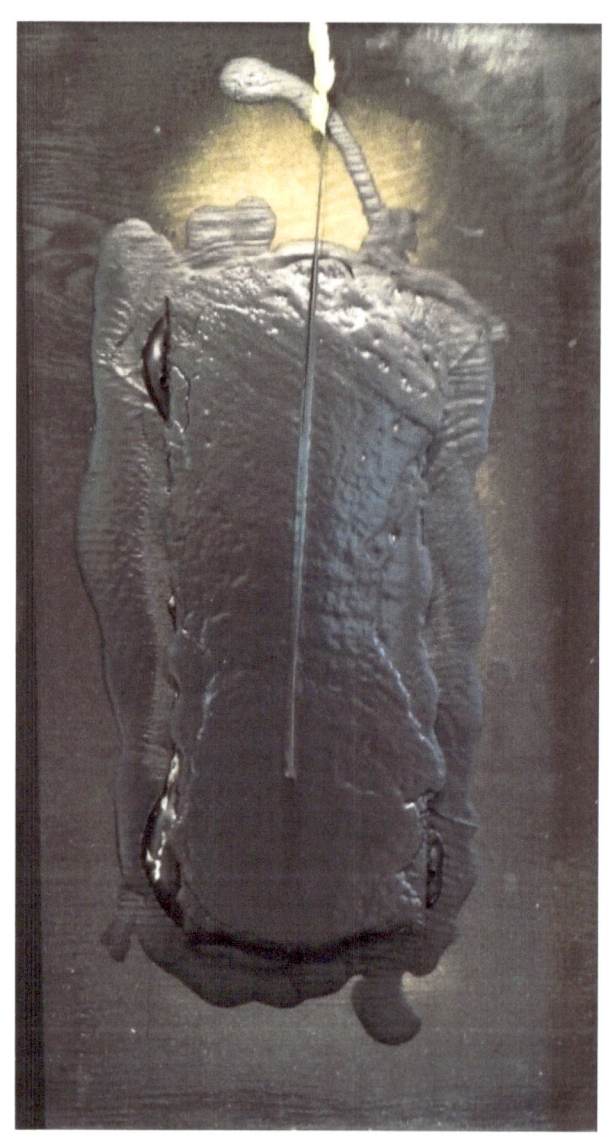

over over over kill

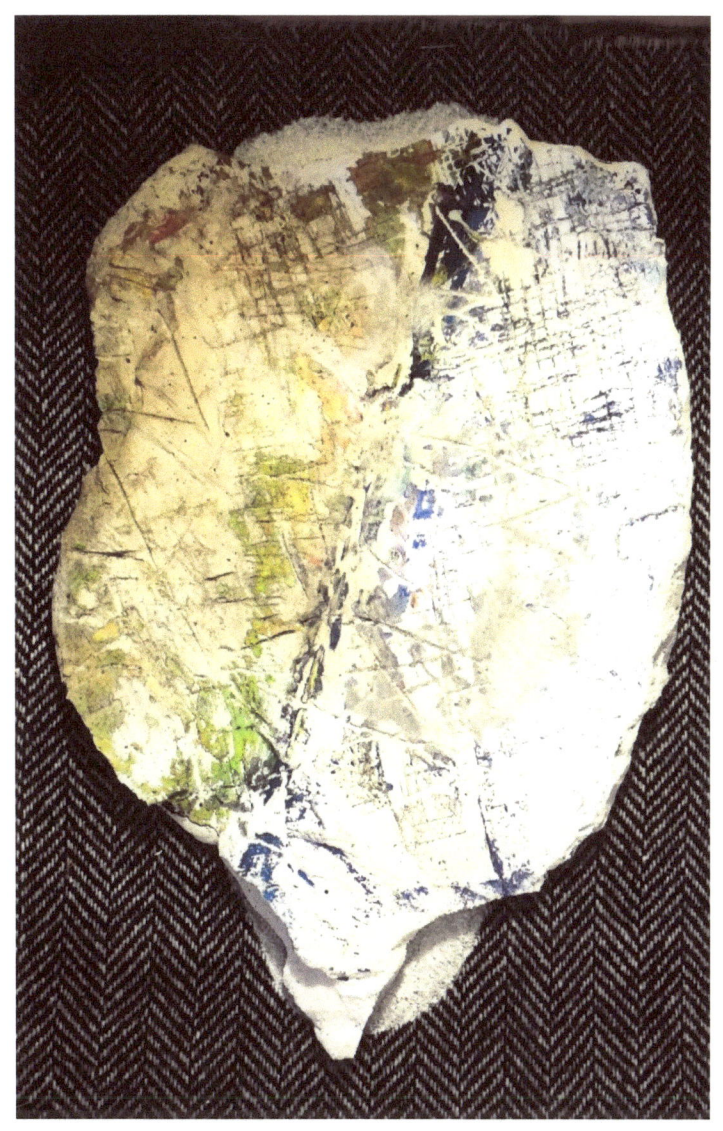

flying high flying low but flying i surely

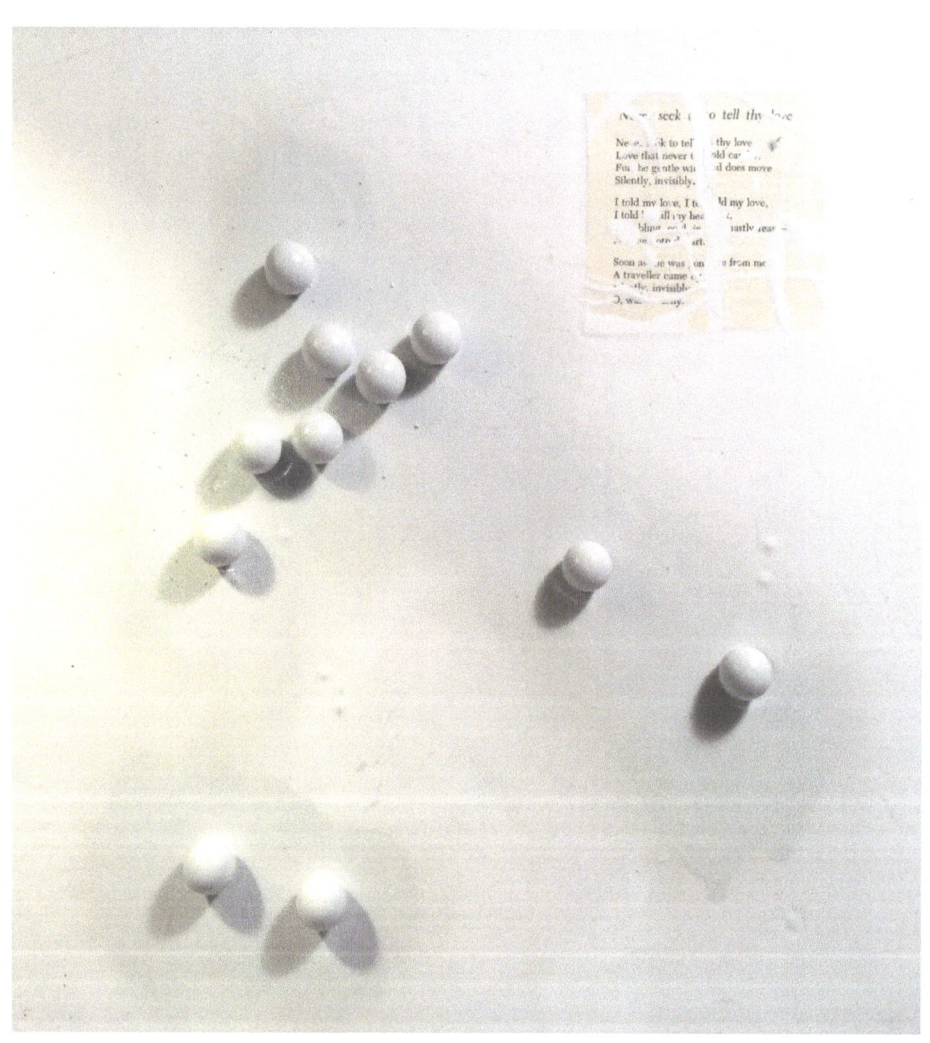

mon pay c'est say l'hiver

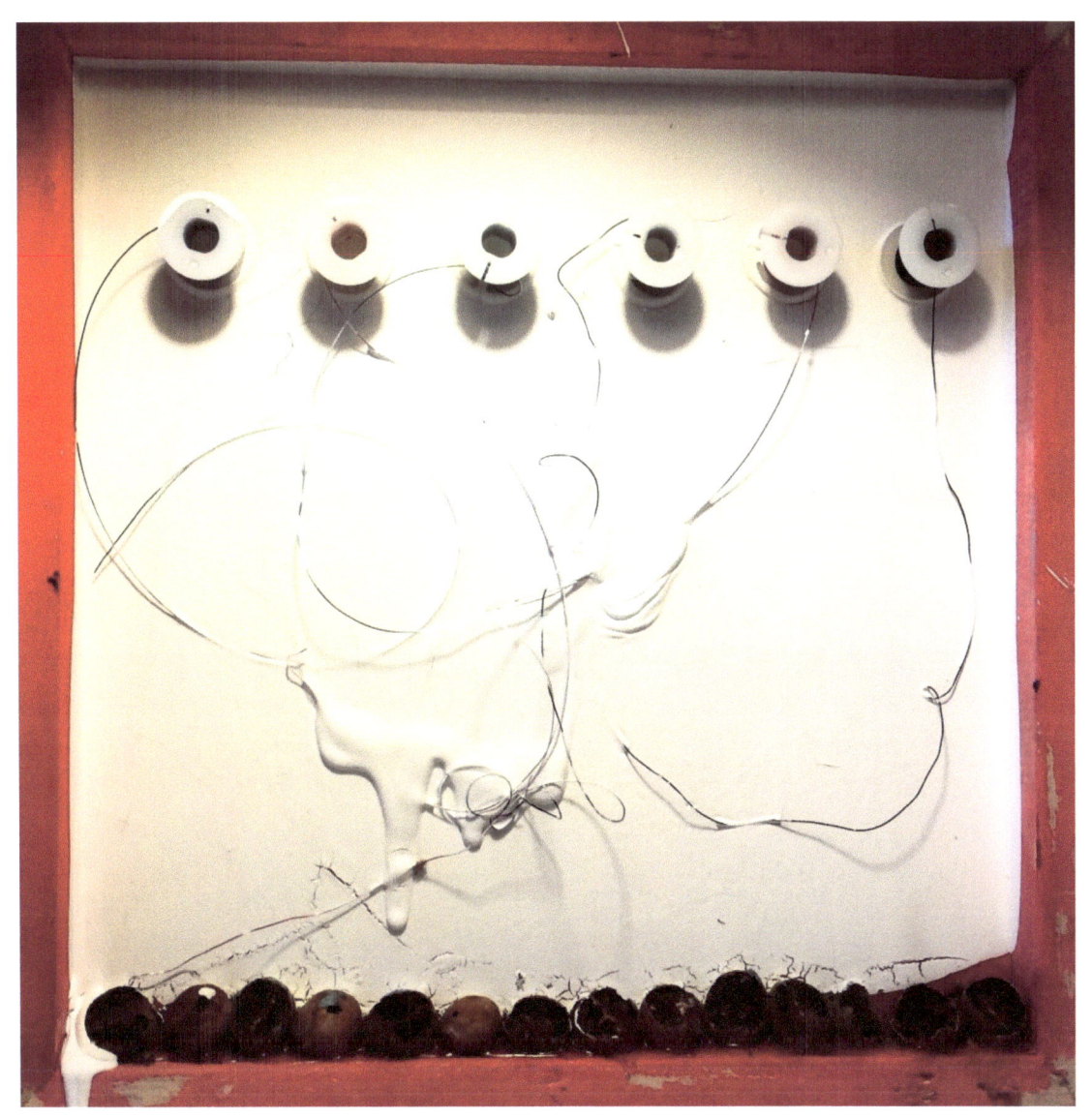

what have 14 acorns got to do with a shock

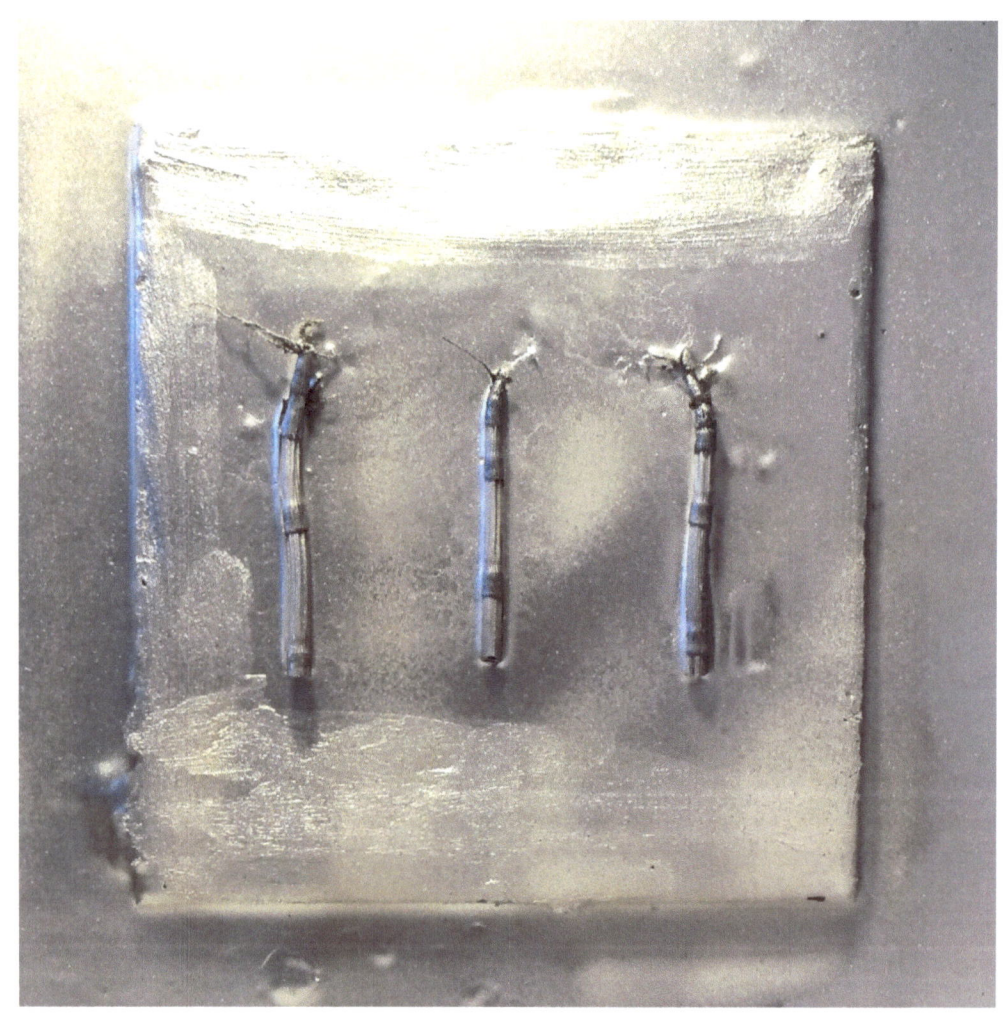

these aren't ice cream cones but the biopsy will tell

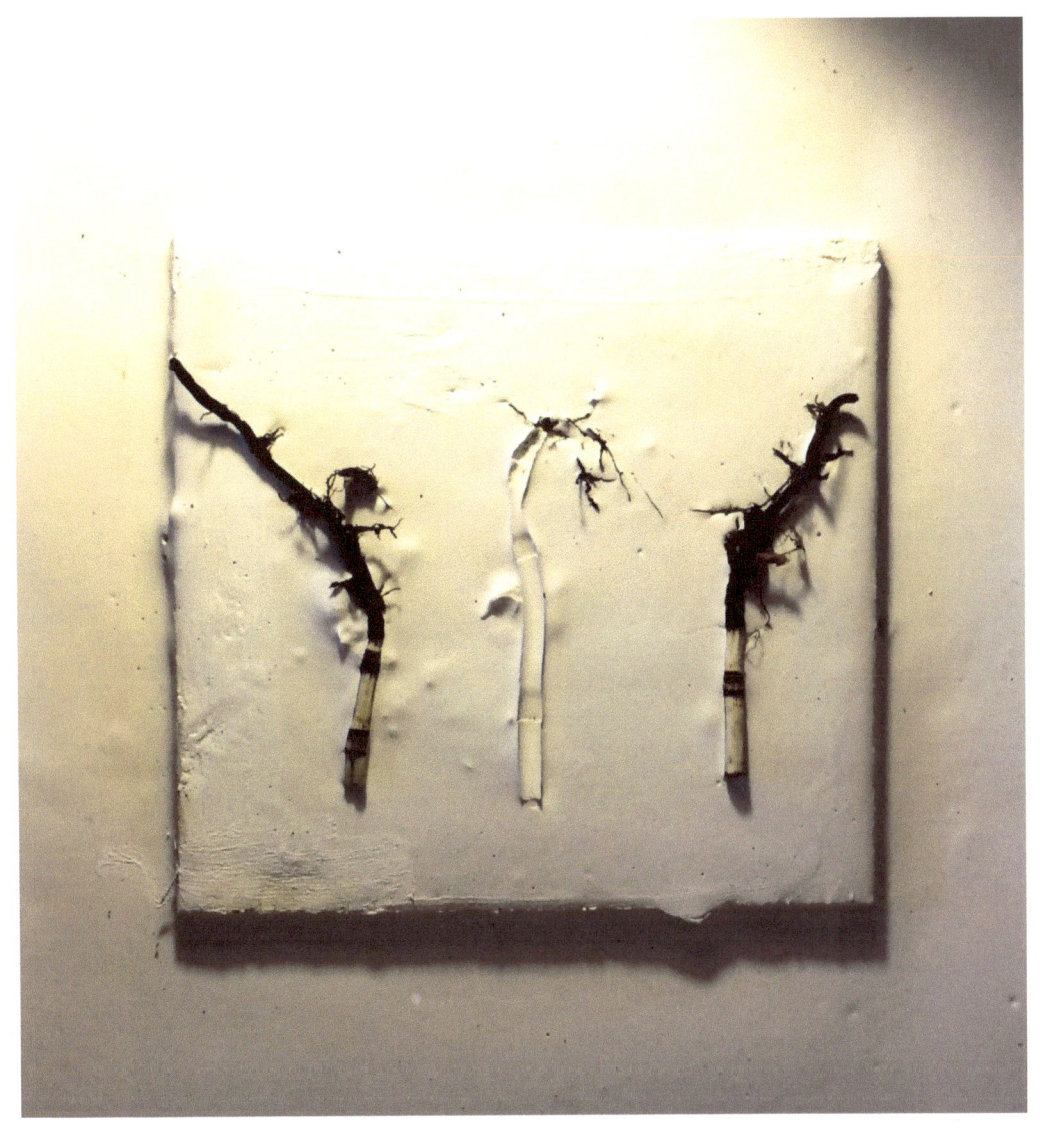

preserved but so what

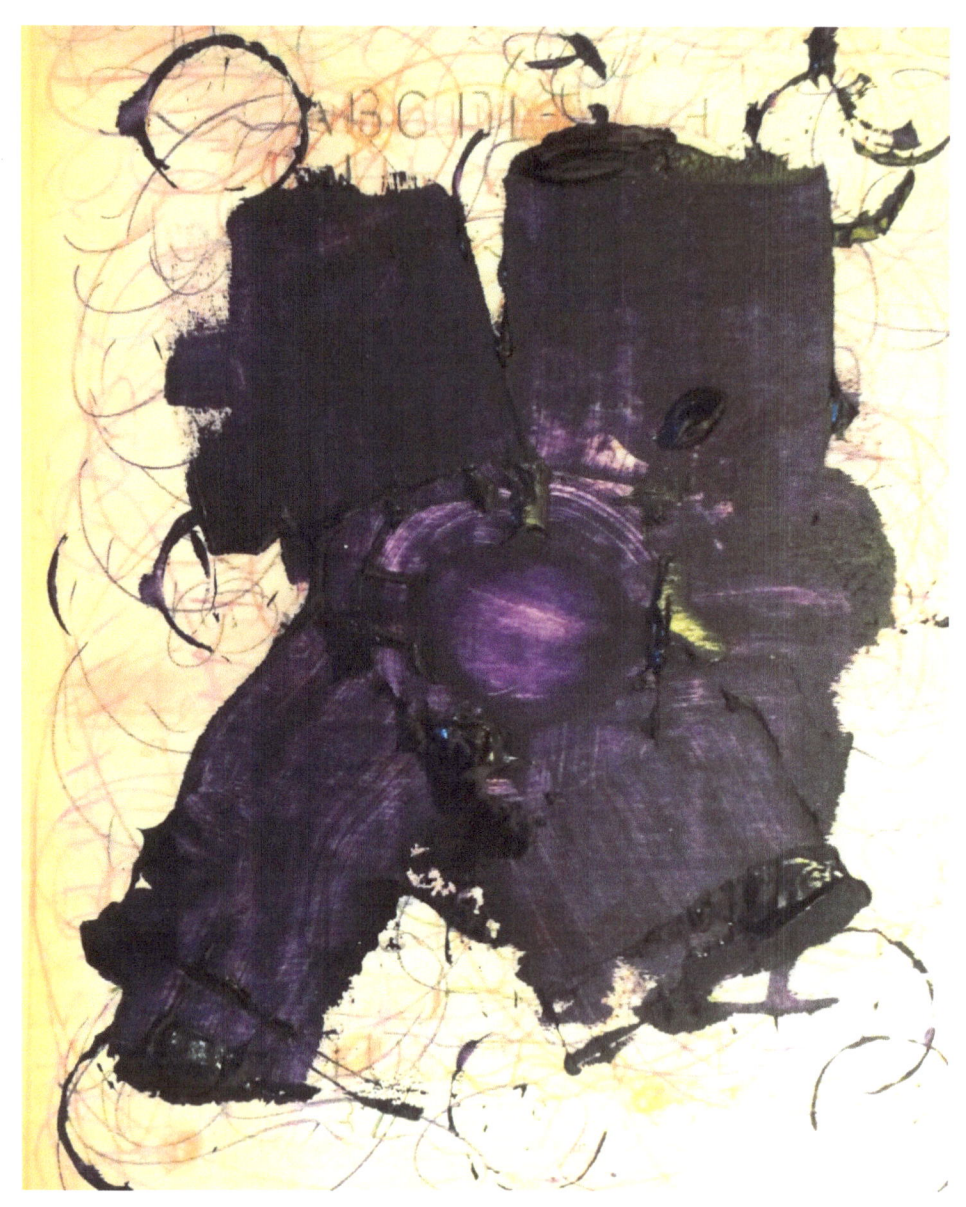

when I was a child I was a child my child

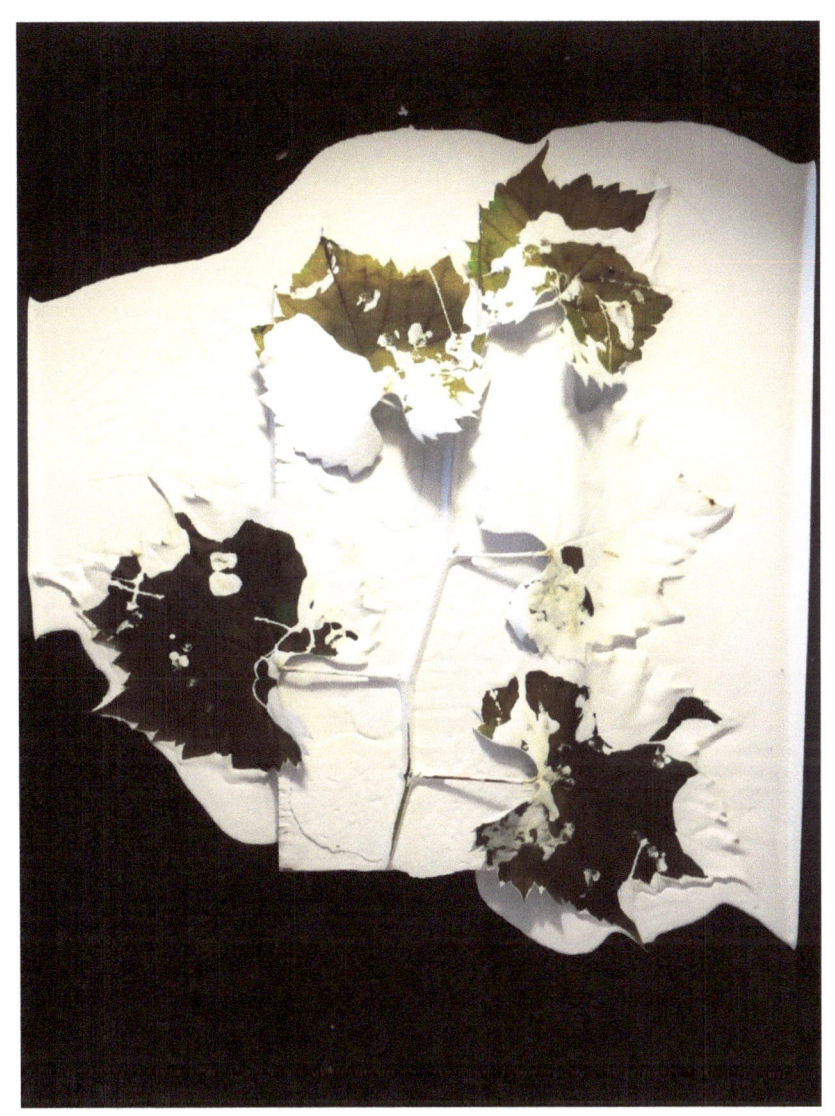

yes that's beautiful

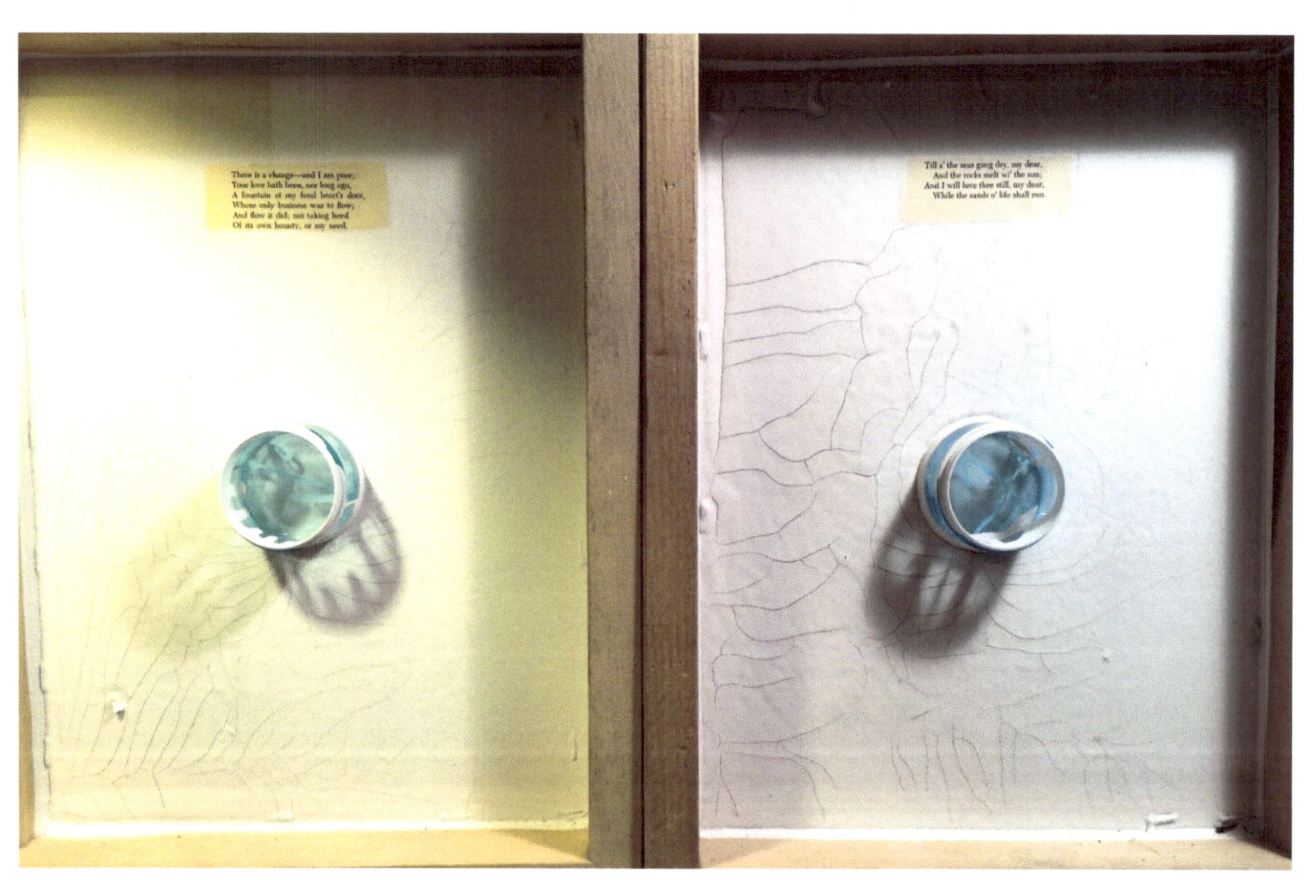

There is a change—and I am poor;
Your love hath been, not long ago,
A fountain at my fond heart's door,
Whose only business was to flow;
And flow it did; not taking heed
Of its own bounty, or my need.

Till a' the seas gang dry, my dear,
And the rocks melt wi' the sun;
And I will luve thee still, my dear,
While the sands o' life shall run.

hot and cold that's easy

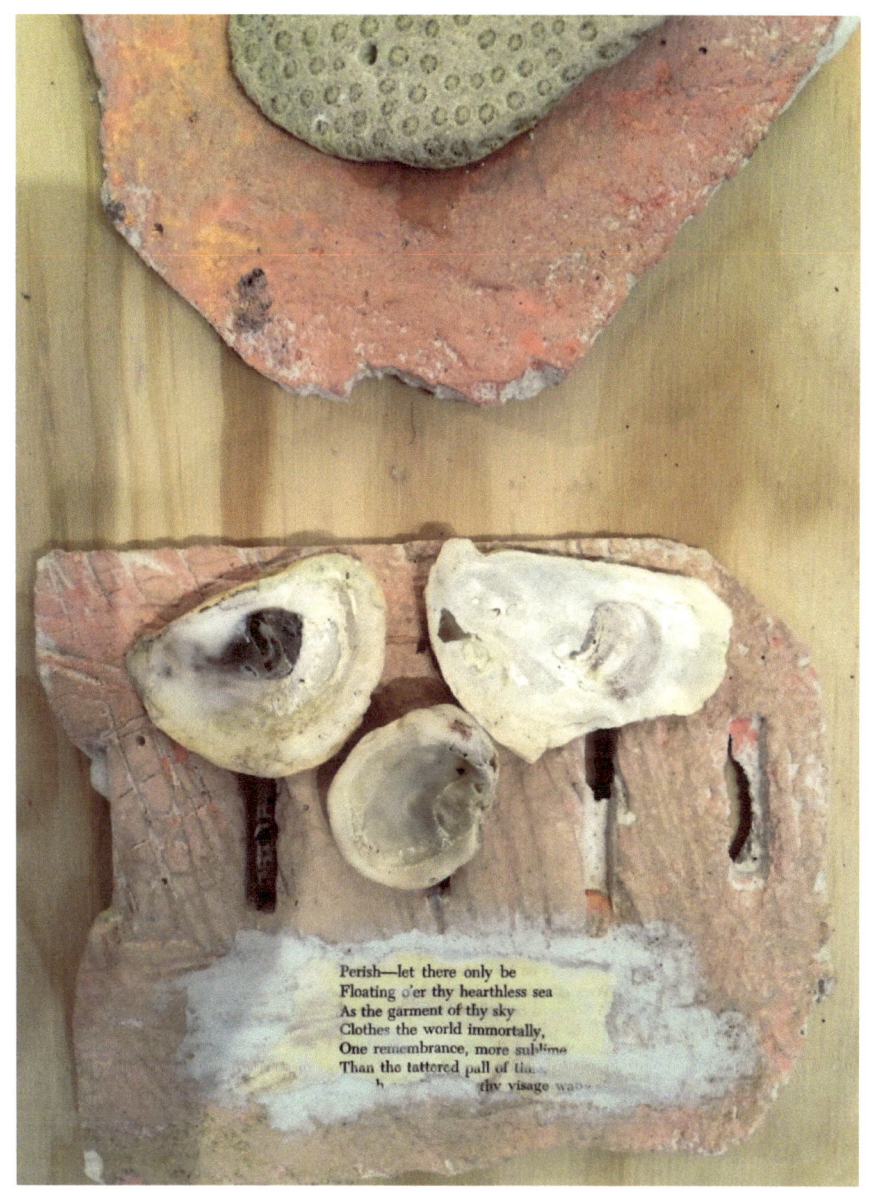

Perish—let there only be
Floating o'er thy heartless sea
As the garment of thy sky
Clothes the world immortally,
One remembrance, more sublime
Than the tattered pall of ti...
h ...... thy visage wao..

i know the words I know the words i know

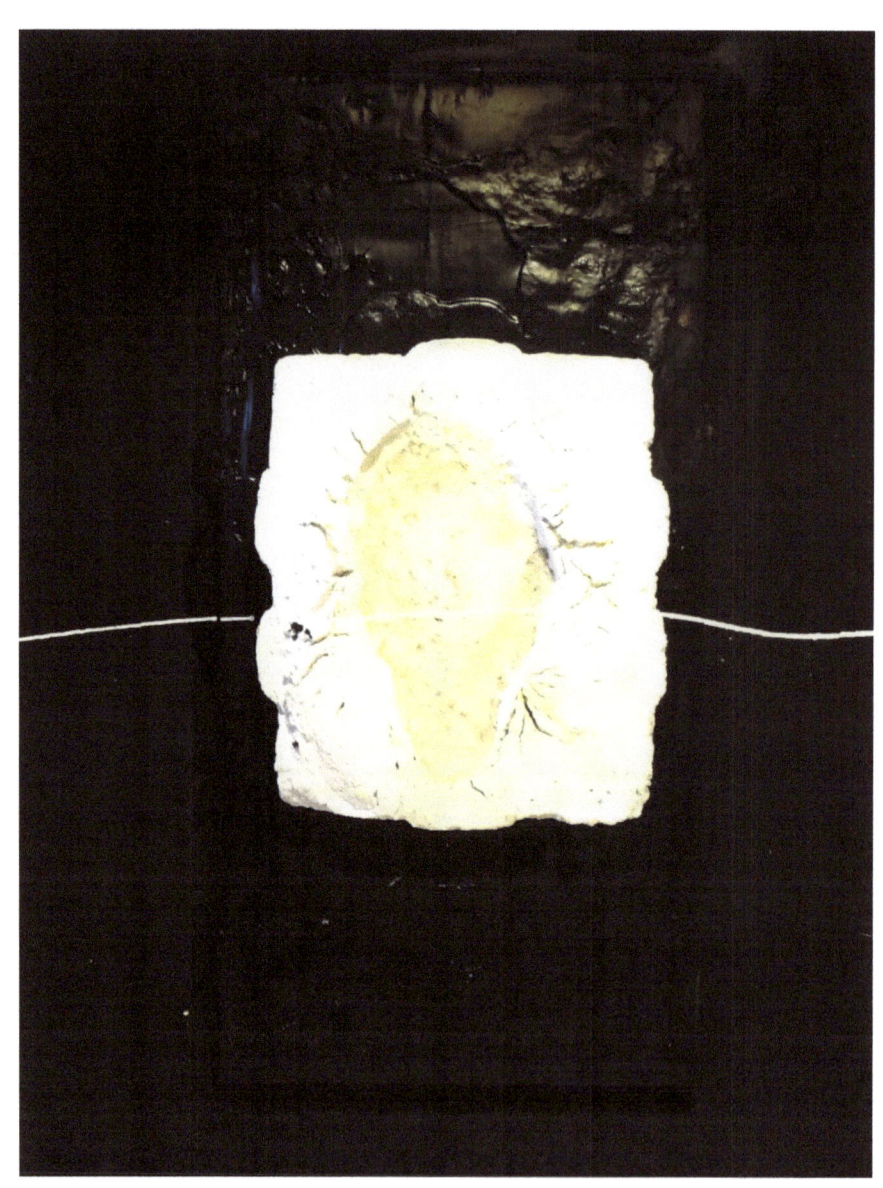

i think yellow

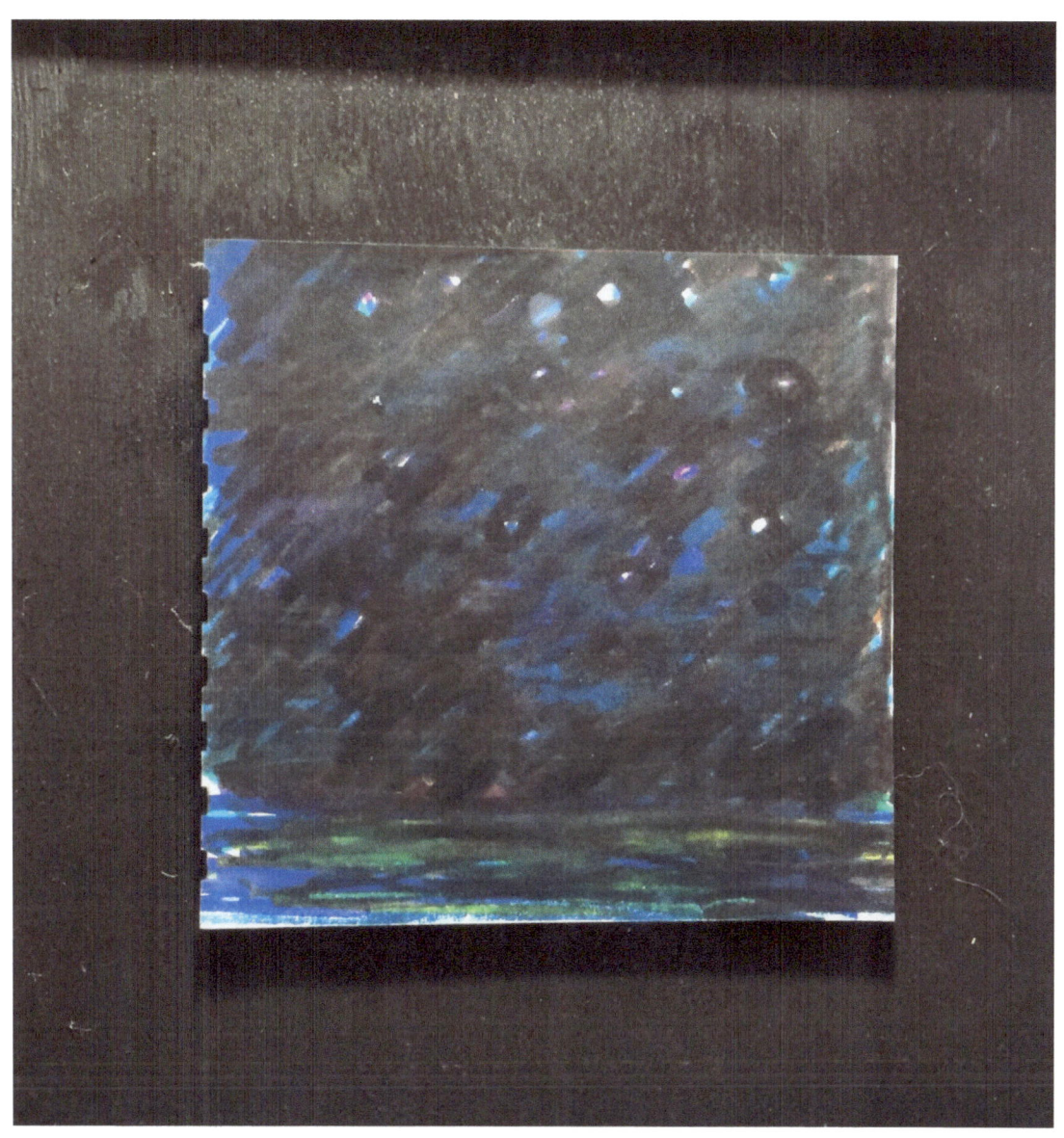

stars yes on the beach with you yes

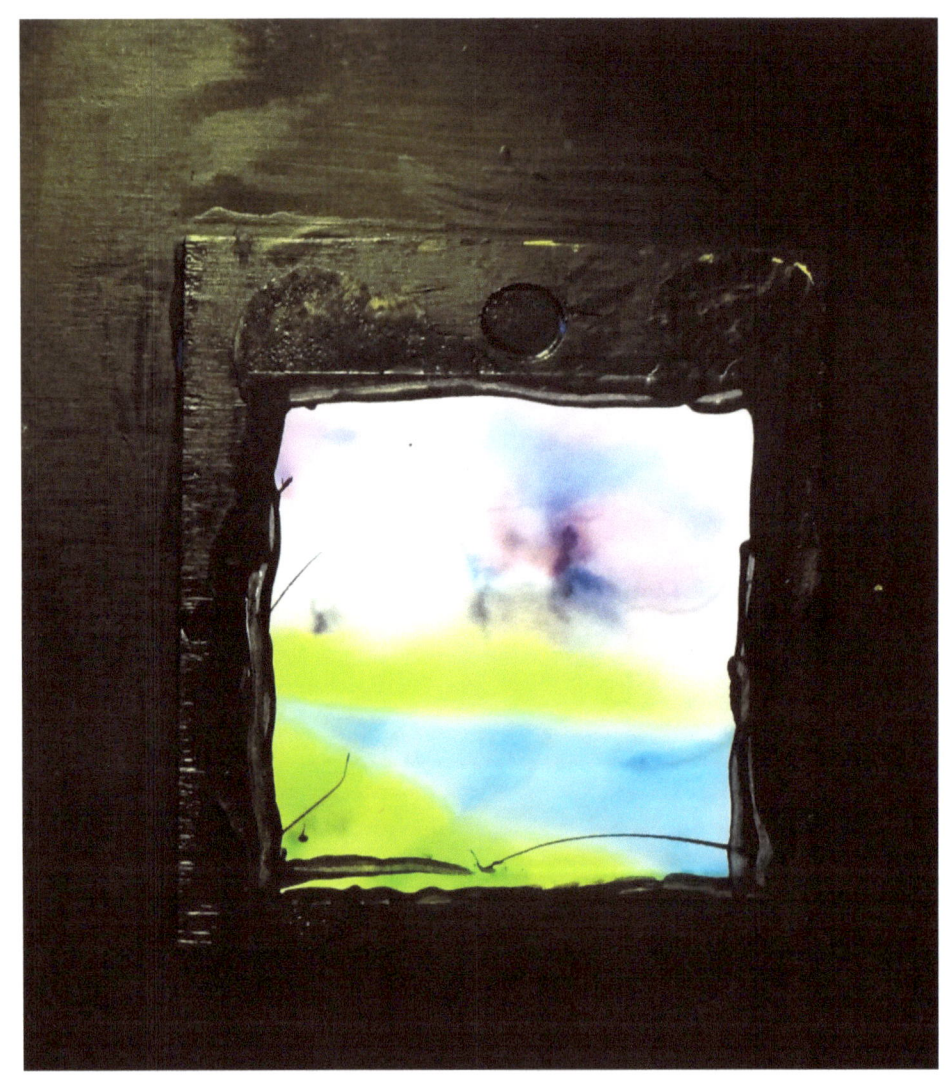

the water is blue but the water is sinking

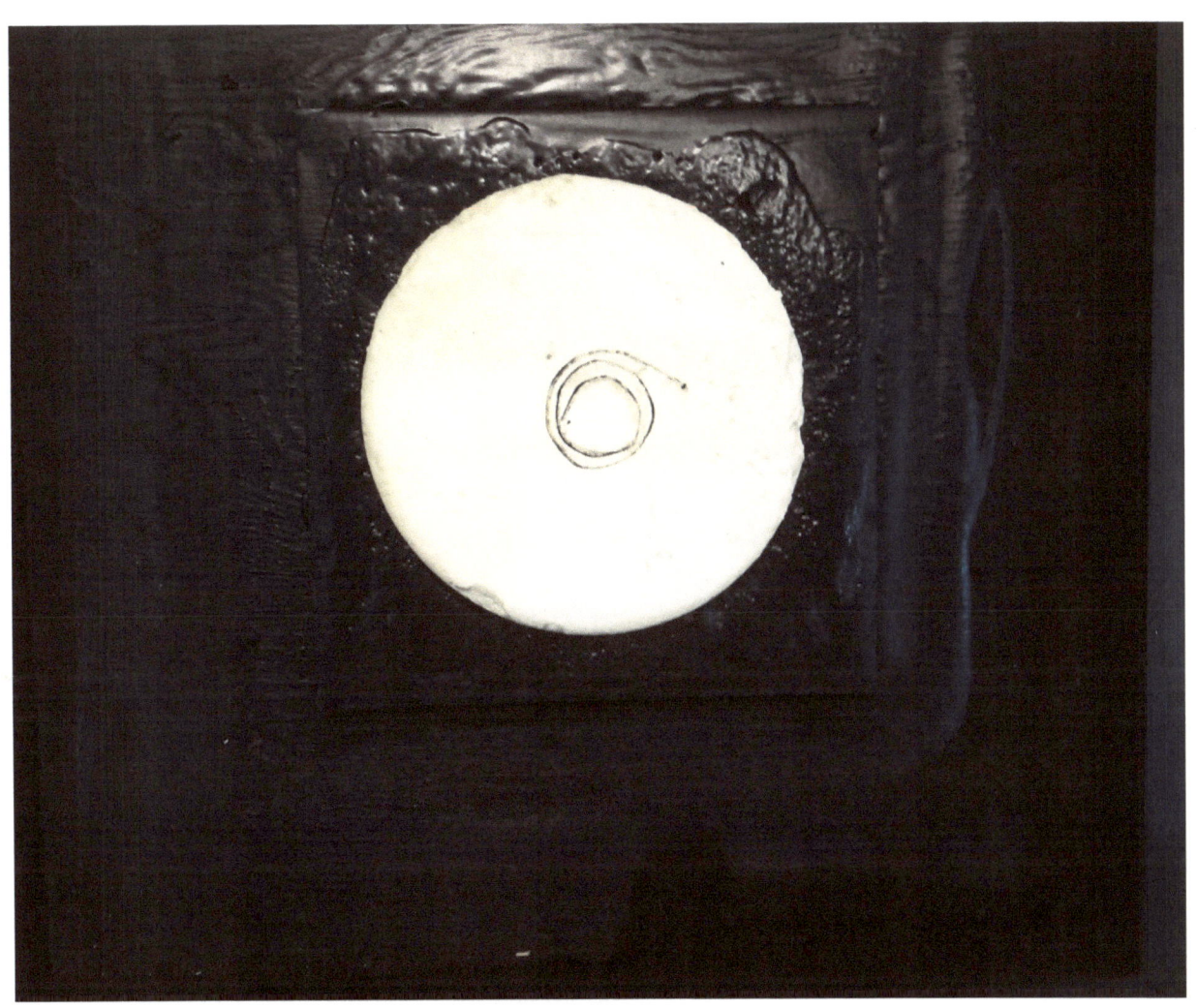

where am i

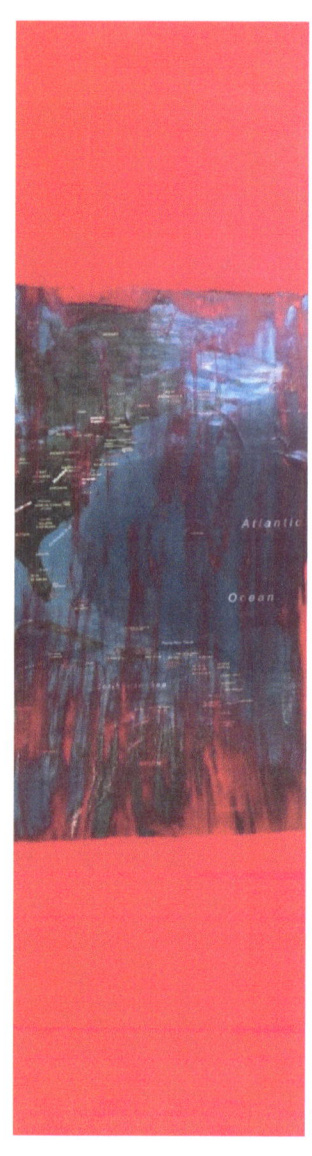

map ocean city fire city ocean ma

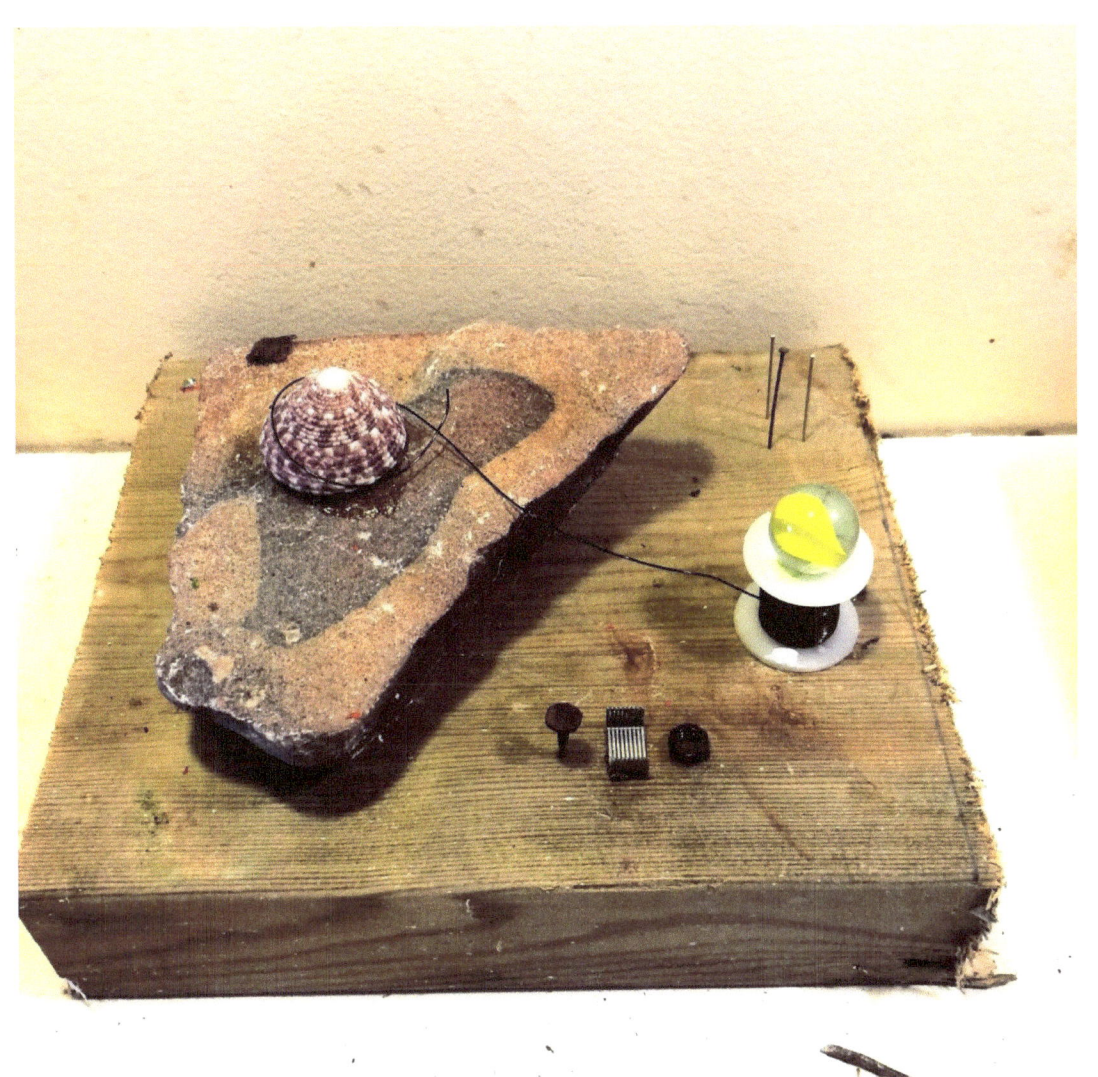

all my own stuff yes your own own please be

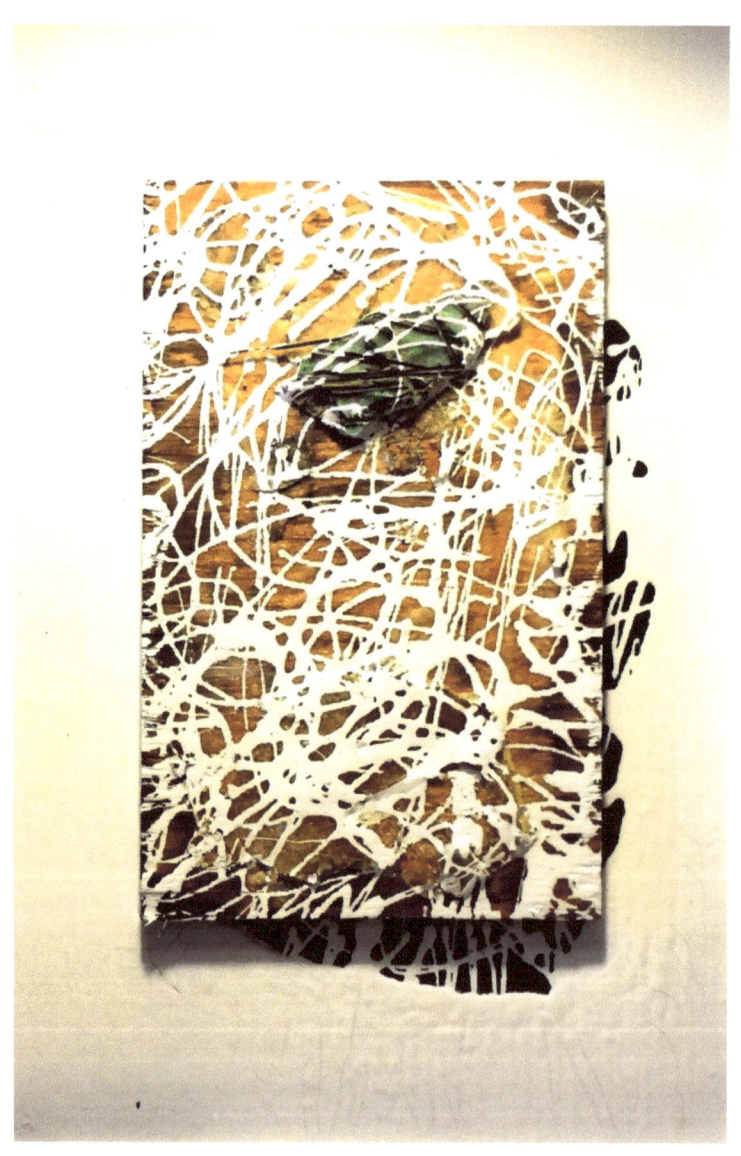

finish the sentence oh but then up and away

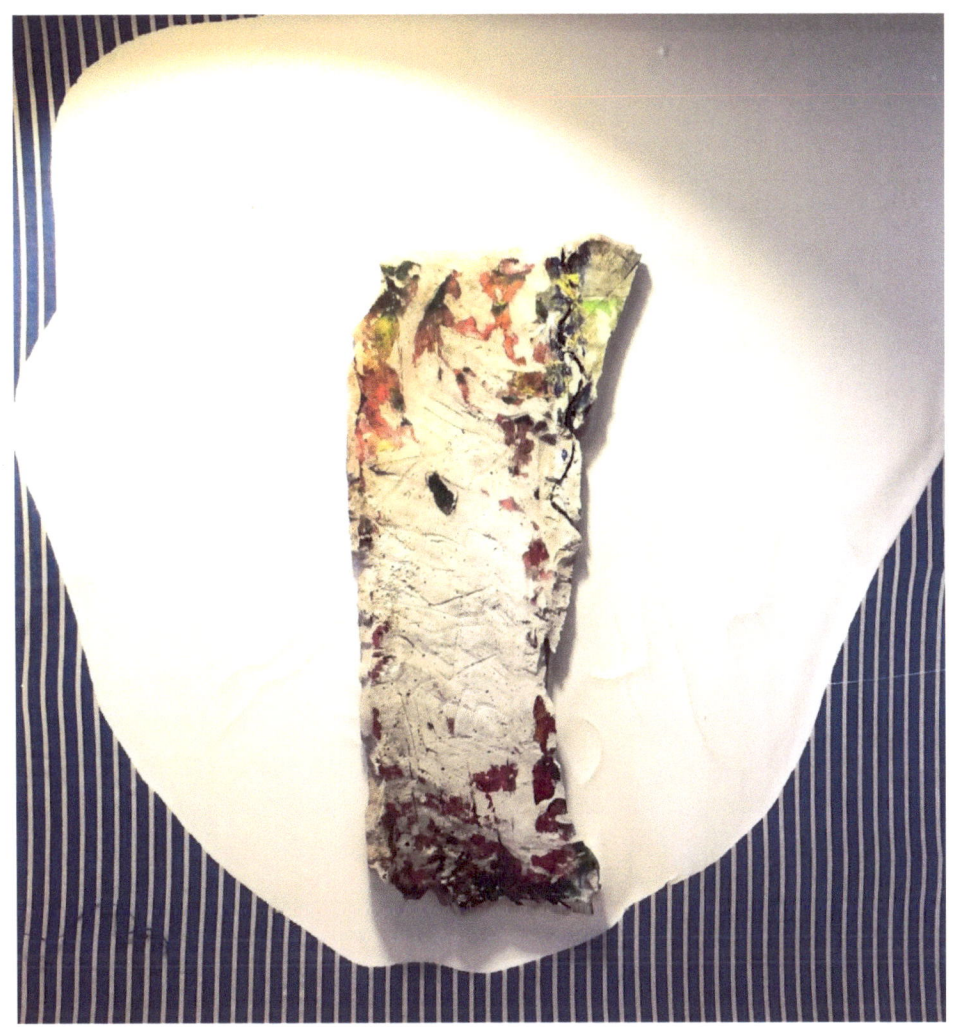

tie tying trying to

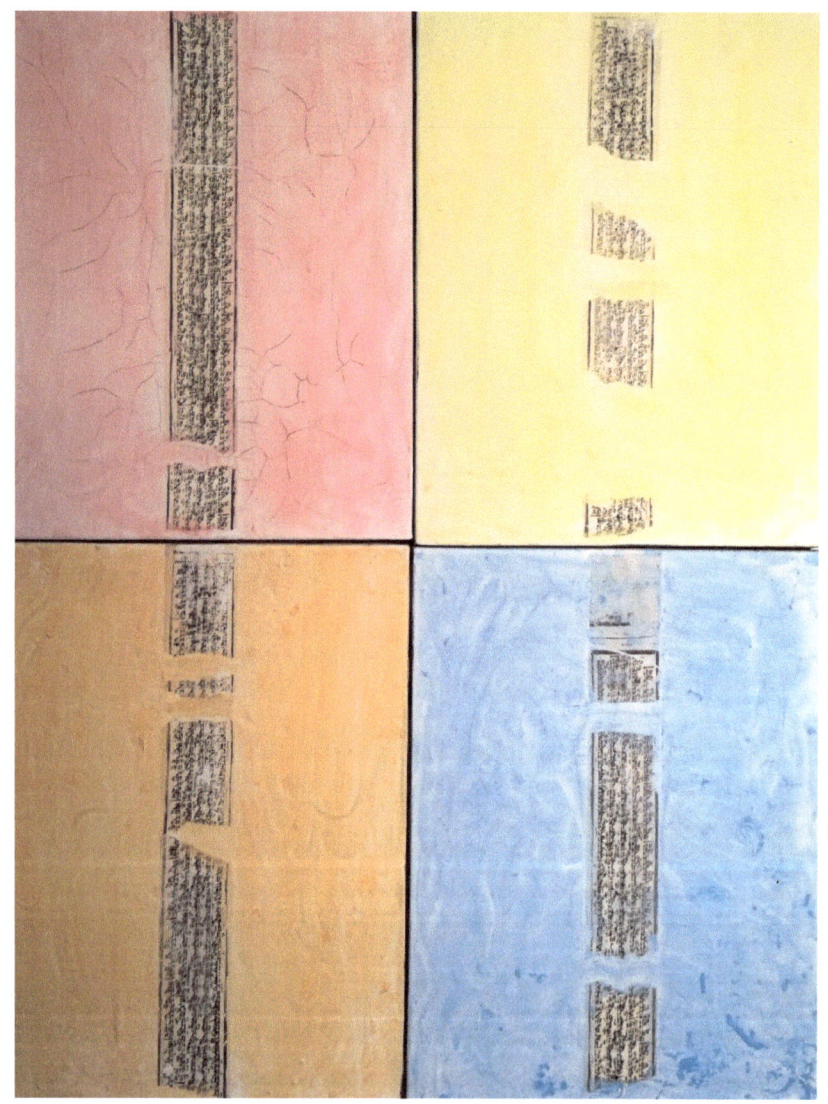

we went to Tibet on the train remember

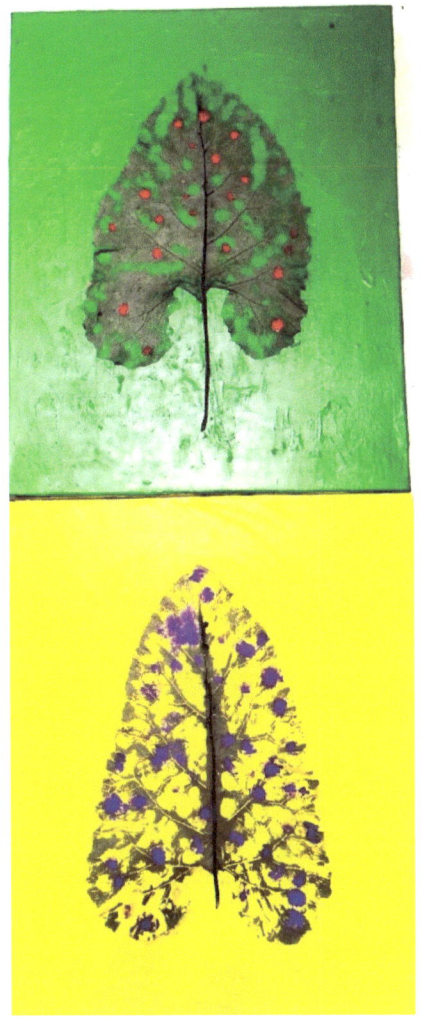

you know everything is connected so so are we

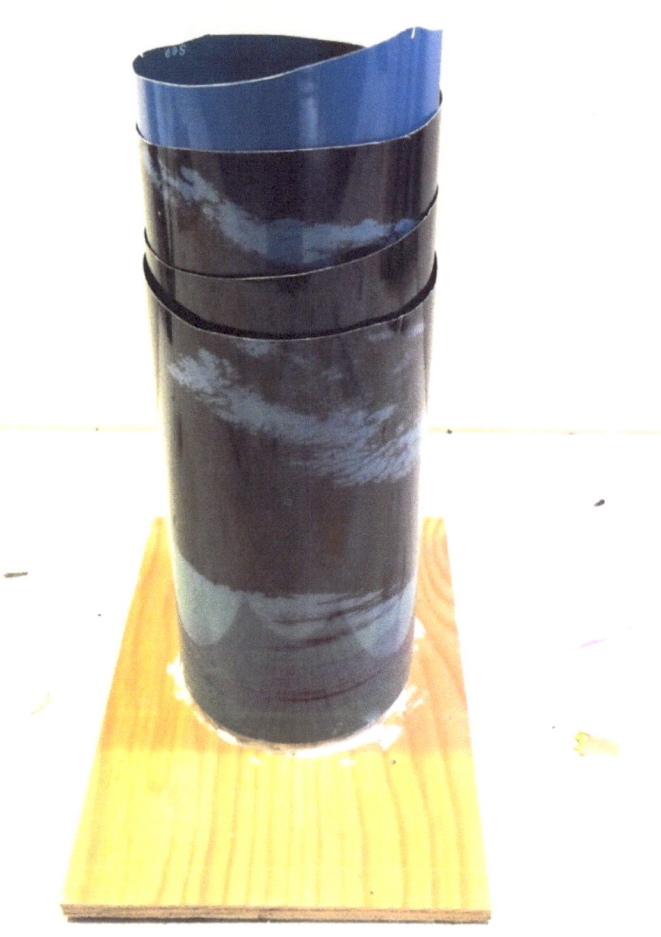

you can roll up the clouds I will for you

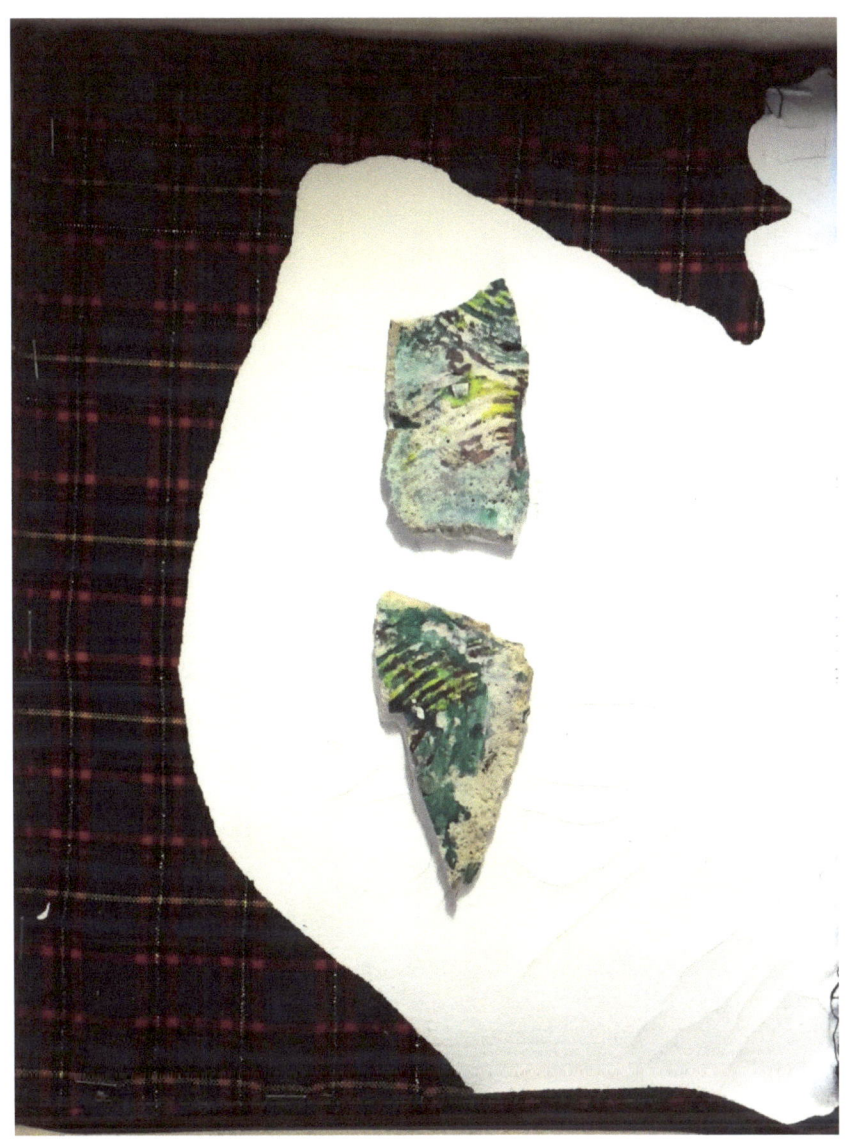

shards sharp front or back

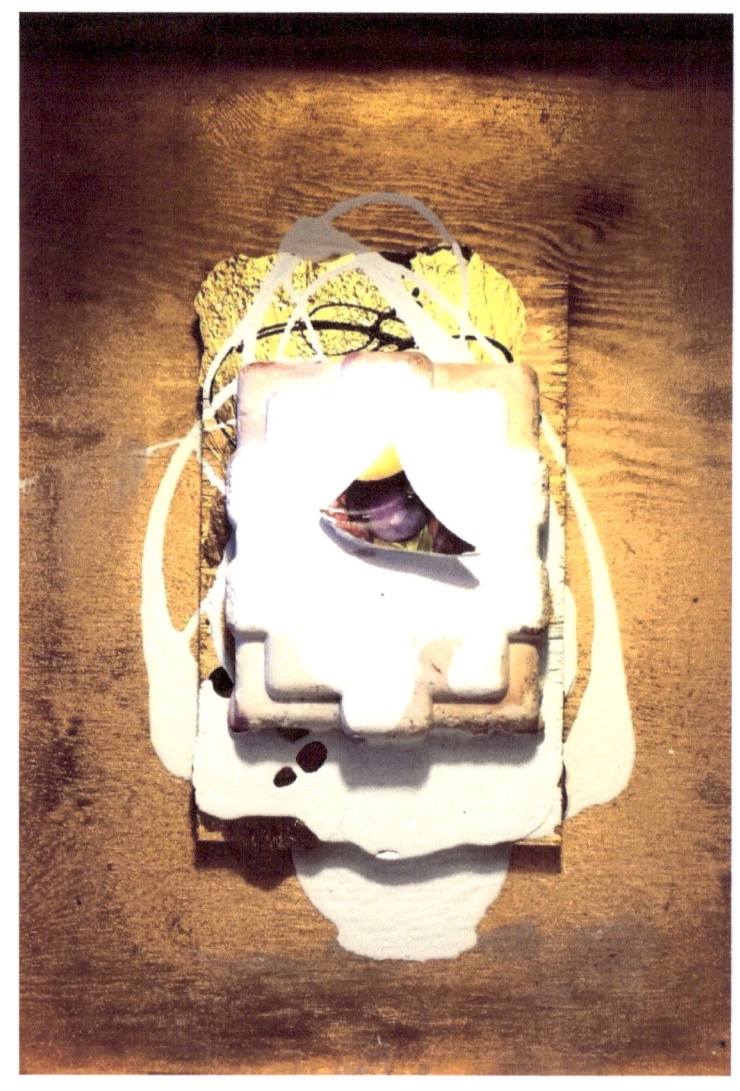

guess

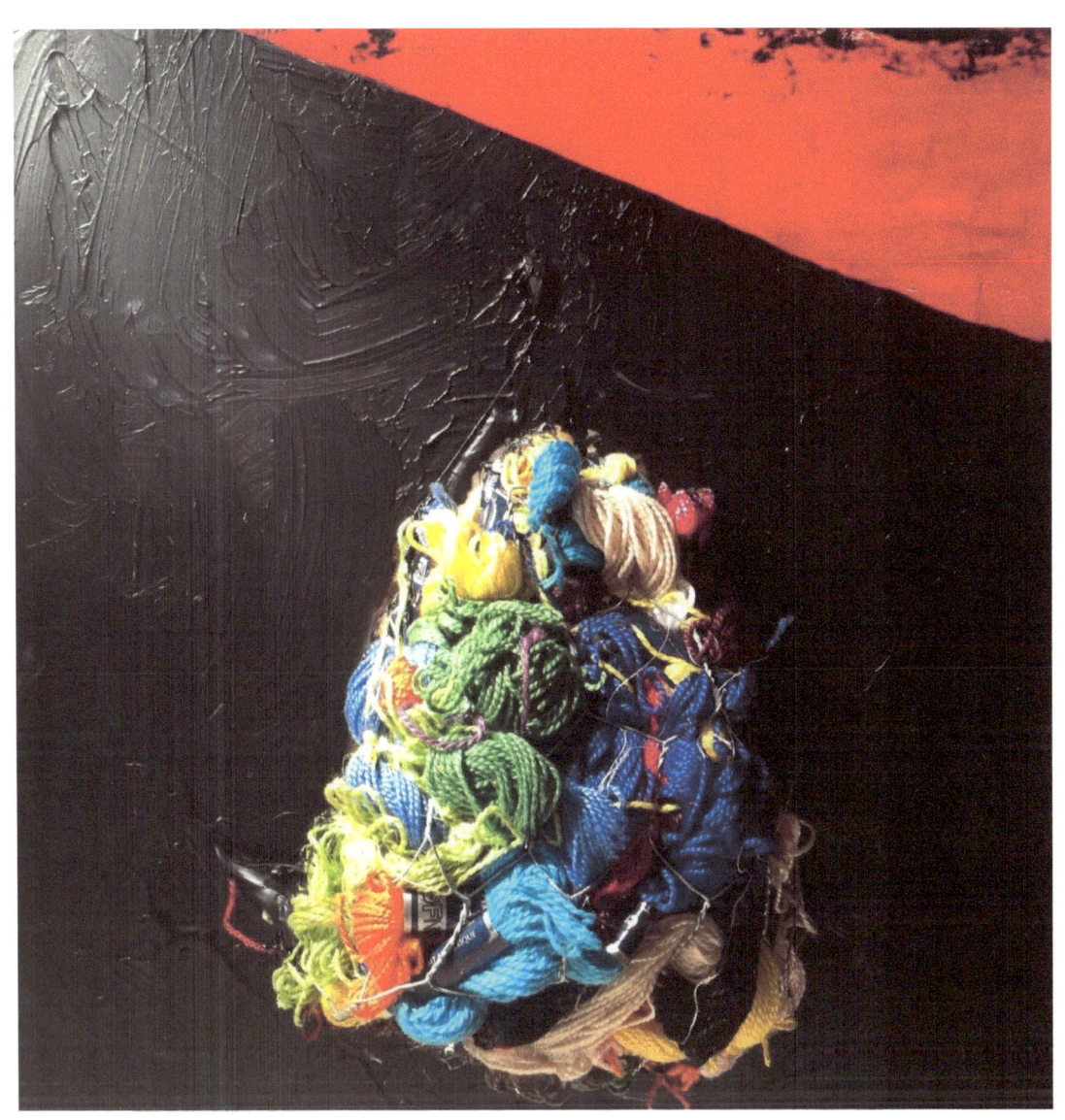

a terrible doom

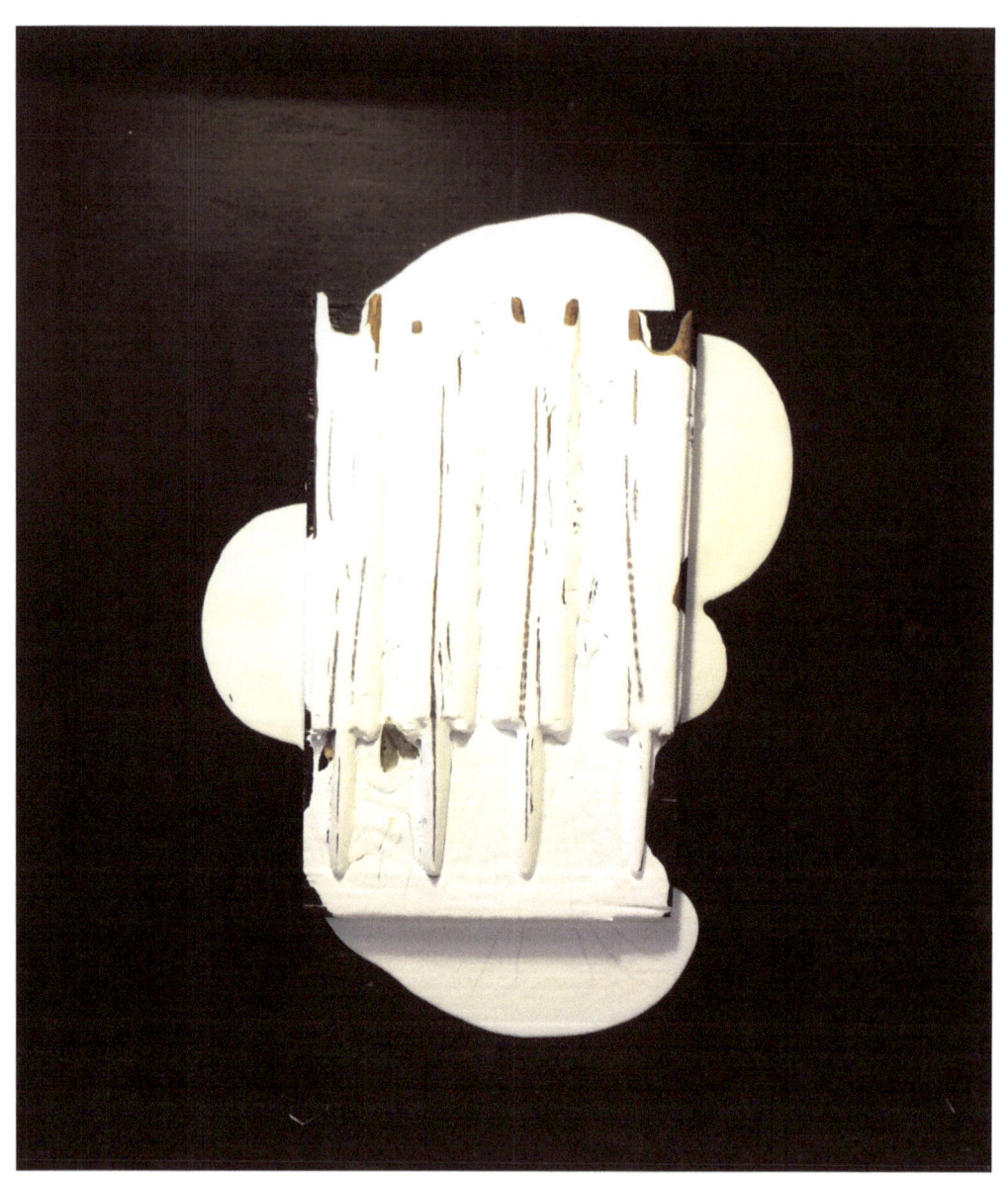

music then at the last

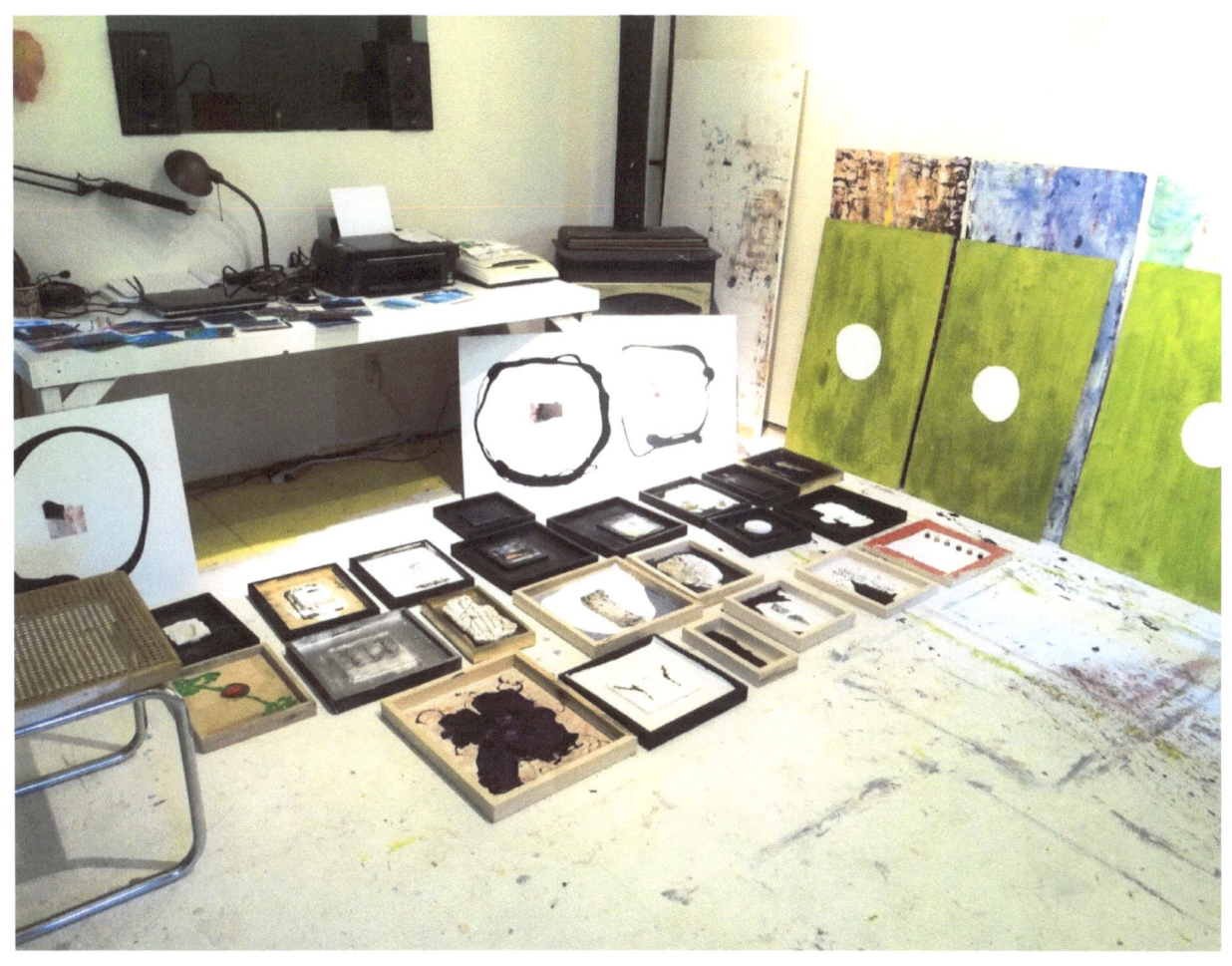

september 2014 or what you will in no space time

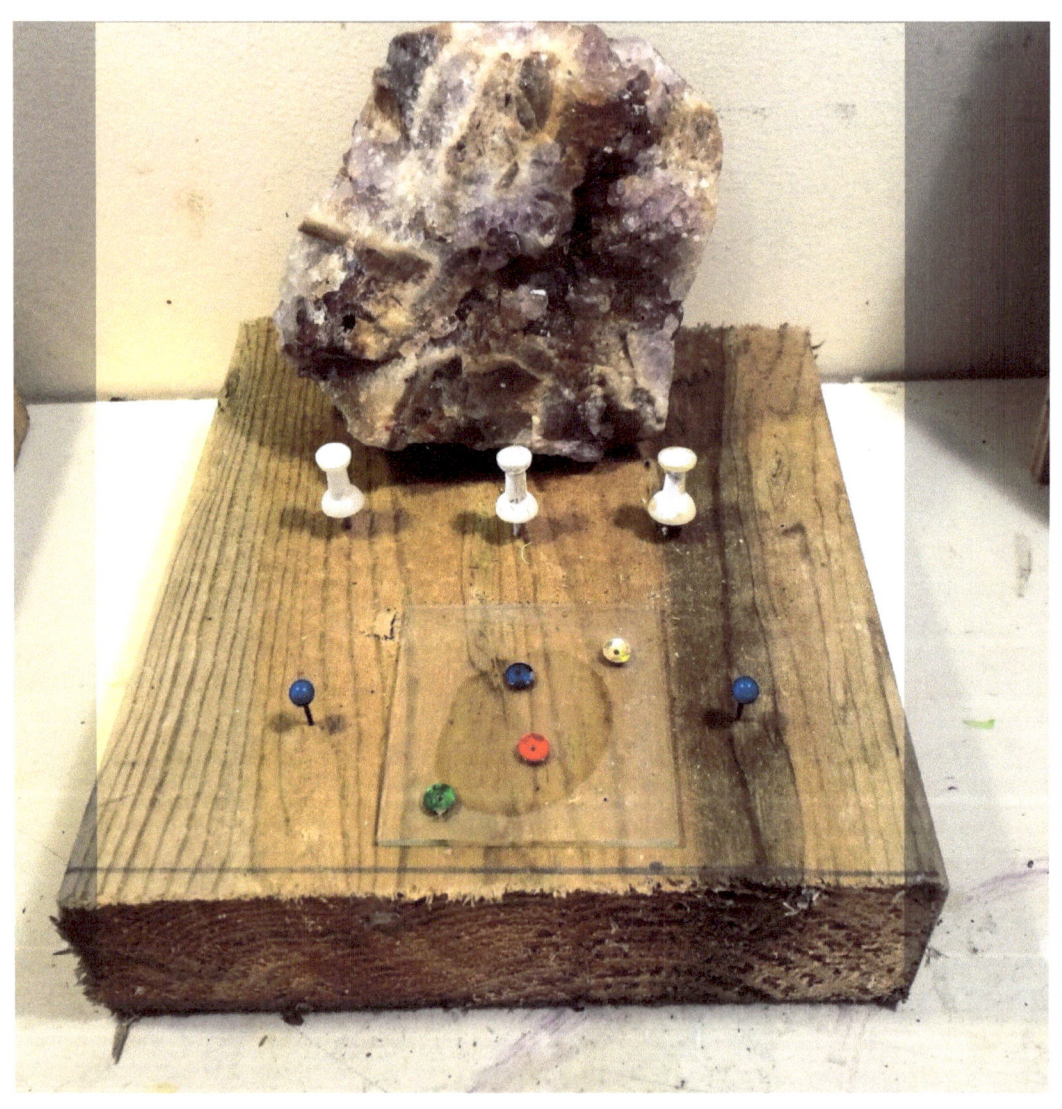

power station for amethyst brain

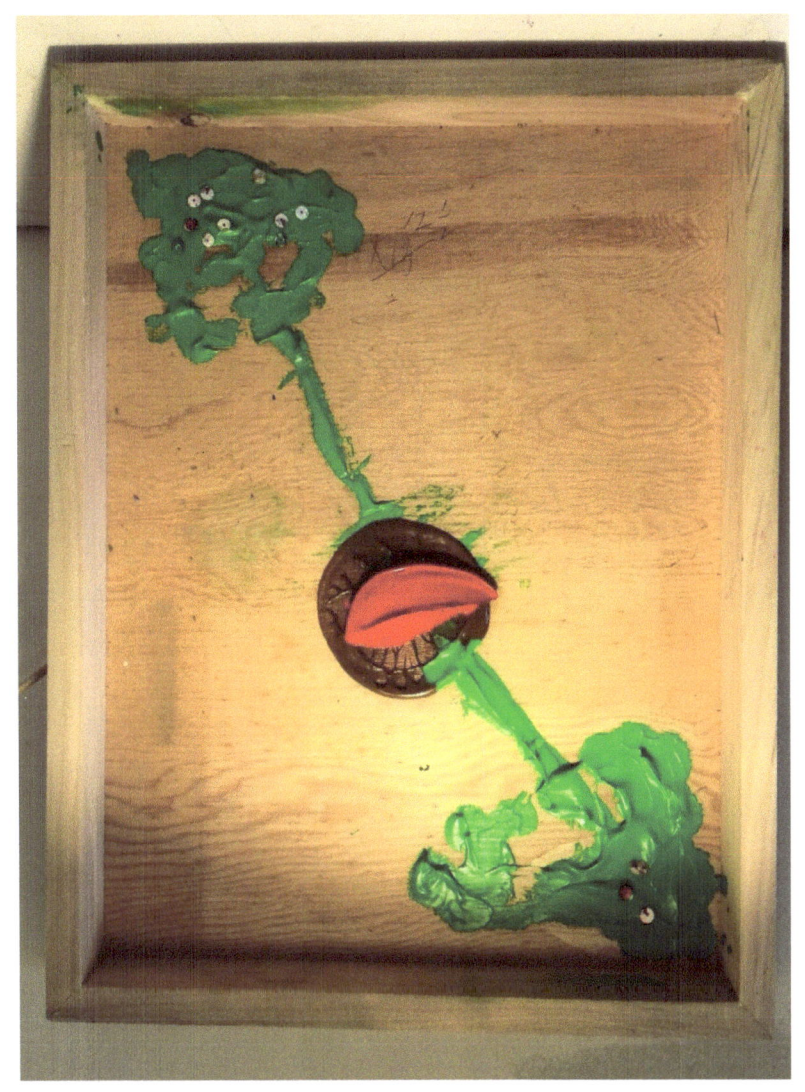

i kiss you you kiss me

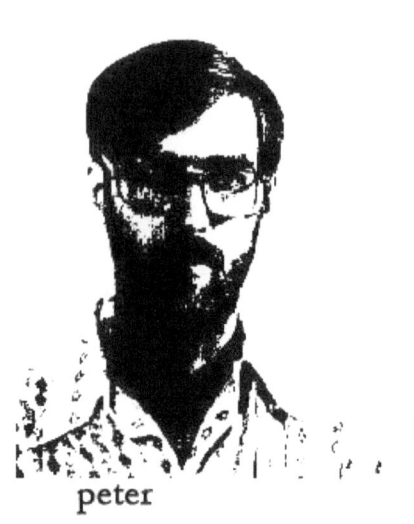

peter

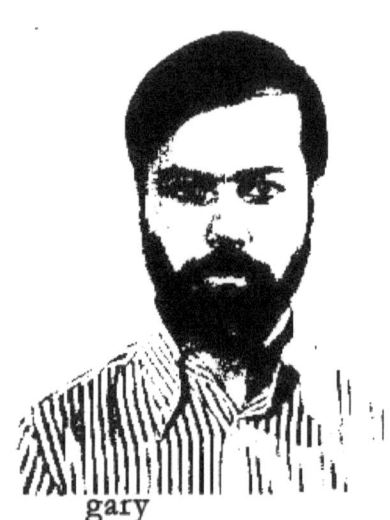

gary

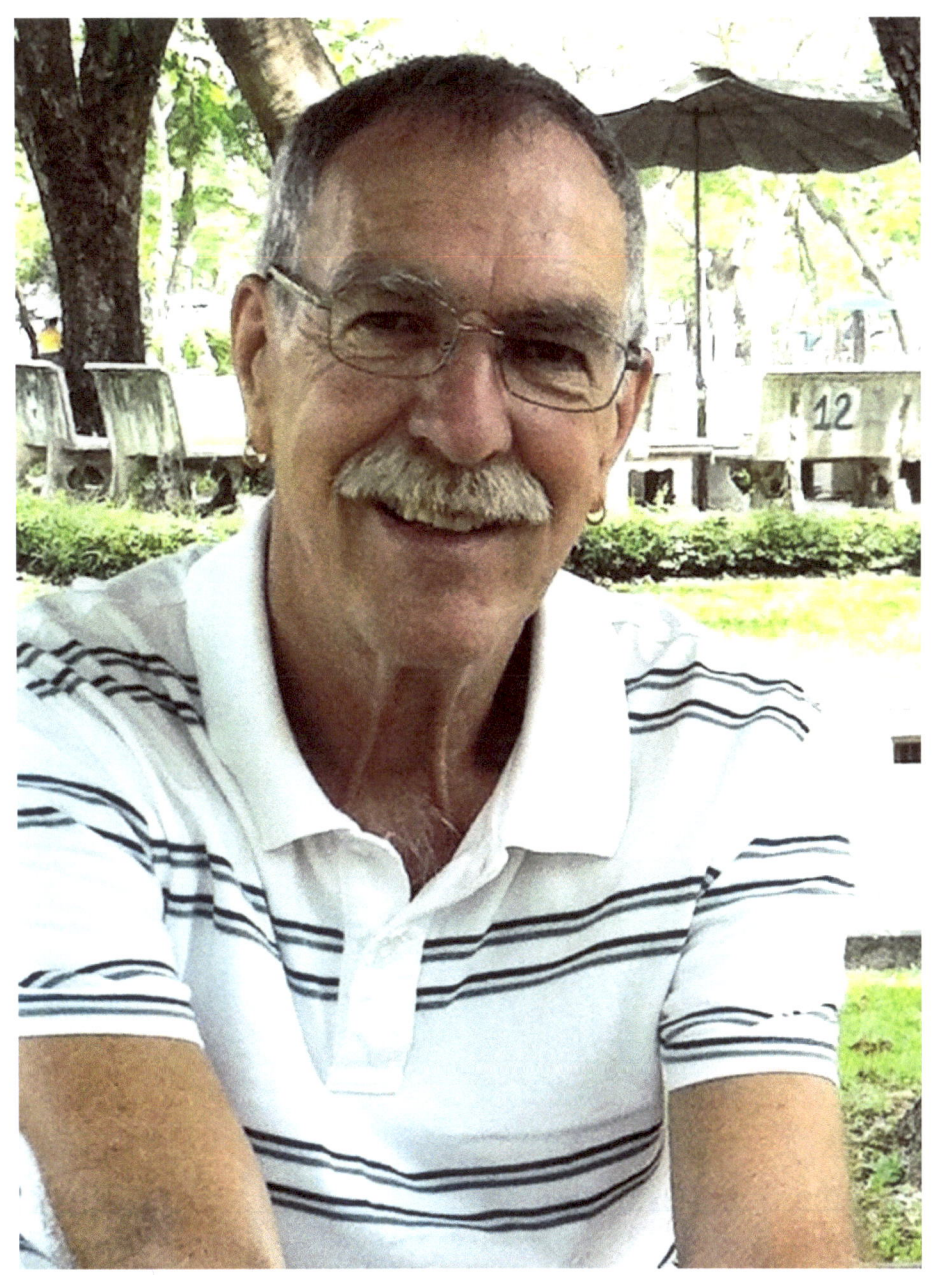

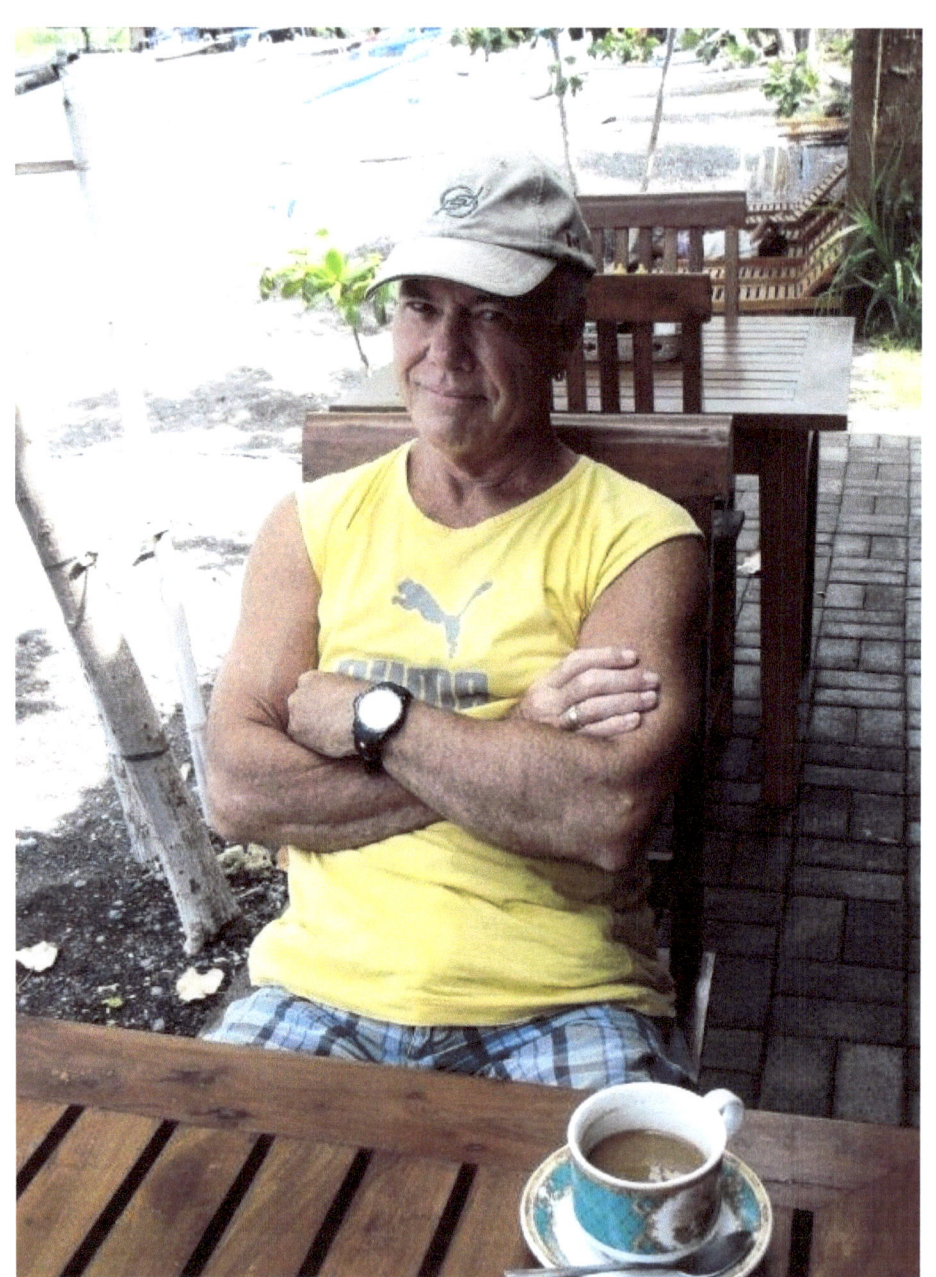